MW00934708

Goal-Oriented Decision Modeling with OpenRules

A Practical Guide for Development of Operational Business Decision Models using OpenRules and Excel

By Jacob Feldman, PhD

ISBN 978-1-7944986-9-3

Copyright © 2019 Jacob Feldman. All rights reserved. Except as permitted under the United States Copyright Act of 1976, no part of this publication may be reproduced or distributed in any form or by any means, or stored in a data base or retrieval systems, without the prior written permission of the copyright holder.

Company and product names mentioned herein are the trademarks or registered trademarks of their respective owners.

Table of Contents

Preface

About Business Decision Modeling. Nowadays Business Decision Modeling is one of the major technological and methodological approaches that support decision making processes across a wide range of business problems from loan origination and insurance underwriting to clinical guidelines and product recommendations. Business decision modeling is oriented to subject matter experts who build and maintain operational decision models incorporated into modern enterprise architectures. A decision model usually has a clearly defined business goal, subgoals, and their representations using decision tables and other forms of executable business rules. With the mass acceptance of the OMG standard "Decision Model and Notation (DMN)" [1] and availability of well-established Business Rules and Decision Management tools [2], business decision modeling became a mainstream approach. This guide introduces a new, goal-oriented approach that essentially simplifies practical decision modeling.

About OpenRules. OpenRules [3] is a highly popular open source Business Rules and Decision Management system used by multiple corporations and government agencies worldwide in real-world production environments since 2004. OpenRules is oriented to subject matter experts who want to build operational decision models for their own business environments. OpenRules utilizes commonly used tools such as MS Excel or Google Sheets as decision model editors and provides powerful rule engines for their execution. A new

Preface

OpenRules Release 7, introduced in 2018, empowers business users with a clear methodology and supporting tools for development of complex, goal-oriented decision models. It provides an essentially enhanced decision engine capable of automatically discovering an execution path for all goals and effectively executing them against input data. OpenRules does not force a human modeler to explicitly define dependencies between goals within a decision model providing a simple yet very powerful way to build and execute decision models.

About this guide. The objective of this guide is to help readers quickly learn how to build efficient and maintainable decision models using a goal-oriented decision modeling approach with OpenRules. Readers learn by examples and may start developing their own decision models without any preliminary knowledge after reading a few opening chapters. This book not only guides readers on how to create working, maintainable decision models but also allows them to test and execute (!) their models using OpenRules software that accompanies this guide.

The guide consists of 6 dialog-sessions, during which AUTHOR and READER are developing decision models in gradually increasing complexity. Together they are freely discussing why and how to build operational decision models, including possible missteps, pitfalls, and alternative approaches. From one decision model to another the AUTHOR walks the inquisitive and receptive READER through different decision modeling concepts and notions. By emphasizing and demystifying especially complicated aspects and directing the READER's attention to special situations that occur in real-world decision modeling, the AUTHOR helps the READER become a professional decision modeler.

Preface

This guide may be considered as a continuation of the book "DMN in Action with OpenRules" [4] that explained how to build DMN-based decision models using OpenRules-6. However, this guide takes advantage of the latest OpenRules release and in a step-by-step manner demonstrates how to build executable decision models using the goal-oriented approach and avoiding unnecessary complicated DMN constructions. There are several good sources [5]-[10] that describe the use of DMN and related methodological approaches to business decision modeling.

How to Use this Guide. It is not necessary to read the entire guide. Even if you read only the *first two dialog-sessions* which that explain how to create and test relatively simple decision models, you will get a good introduction to practical decision modeling techniques and may start developing your own models.

The *dialog-sessions 3, 4, and 5* give you more examples of real-world decision models that are implemented using more advanced decision modeling techniques. And, finally, you can look at the *dialog-session 6* only if you want to learn how to build and organize a library of domain-specific decision models that can be used to assemble new decision models by applying the goal-oriented approach.

Each dialog-session starts with a list of discussed topics, and you may skip sessions that are of no interest to you. So, you can read dialog-sessions in the presented order, or you may read them in accordance with your actual interest and needs.

As you go through this guide, you may use Microsoft Excel to create and enhance business decision models. Instead of Excel you may use Google Sheets or Open Office.

Preface

You also may open OpenRules Analyzer in your favorite browser to select, analyze, and test the discussed decision models online without any downloads or installations.

If you want to download the discussed decision models to your own computer to modify and execute them locally, you may get an OpenRules Evaluation Version that already includes all working models in the workspace "openrules.models". Visit http://openrules.com/Book.htm.

Acknowledgments. First, I'd like to acknowledge very helpful comments on the draft of this book I received from Dr. Bob Moore, Rick Schreiber, and Grammarly.

Our customers around the globe use OpenRules day-in and day-out to make better operational business decisions for more than 15 years. Based on this experience, our team added many new features requested from the "trenches" while trying not to over-complicate our product. The new goal-oriented approach is also based on the real-world experience that helped us understand what is really important when our customers build and maintain operational decision models. So, I want to thank all OpenRules customers with whom we have been fortunate enough to work. I hope our existing and new customers will also appreciate the power and simplicity of the new OpenRules approach to decision modeling.

Jacob Feldman, PhD
OpenRules, Inc., CTO
Monroe, New Jersey
February 2019

Dialog-Session 1: Introducing Major Concepts using Decision Model "Vacation Days"

Discussed Topics:
Problem Description
Starting with Glossary
Specify Business Goals and Subgoals
Single-Hit and Multi-Hit Decision Tables
Goal-Oriented Approach to Decision Modeling
Rules Repository
Creating Test Cases
Building Decision Model
Executing Test Cases
Rules Repository
Explanation Reports
Suggested Exercise
Related OpenRules Projects:
VacationDays

AUTHOR. Today is our first session that should become a practical introduction to business decision modeling. During our preliminary meeting, you told me that you've already looked at with several business rules tools and even read a bit about the DMN (Decision Modeling and Notation) standard. Now you want to start building decision models for your own business problems.

READER. Yes, but I have difficulty grasping exactly what decision models are and how I can create working models myself.

AUTHOR. Many business analysts or subject matter experts initially face the same issue. I believe the best solution is to create several simple decision models that you can execute and analyze. Today we'll specify and build a relatively simple but complete decision model that will allow us to introduce the major decision modeling constructs. When we learn new things, you need to have something tangible that you can "touch" and evaluate from different perspectives. So, at the end of today's session, you will be able to "touch" a decision model that we will build and test together using mainly Excel.

READER. I'd love to "touch" and to play with a real decision model.

AUTHOR. OpenRules provides many sample decision models in the downloadable folder "openrules.models" that contains all you need to create and execute your own decision models. We will create all our models using mainly Excel files placed inside subfolders of "openrules.models".

Problem Description

AUTHOR. We will start with the following real-world business decision problem. Imagine that you need to help your organization to automatically calculate a number of vacation days for every employee. This problem was initially specified by Prof. Jan Vanthienen and was implemented by many vendors as a DMCommunity.org Challenge. Here are the business rules:

*Every employee receives at least **22** vacation days.*
Additional days are provided depending on age and years of service:
1) *Only employees younger than 18 or at least 60 years, or employees with at least 30 years of service will receive an **extra 5 days**;*

2) *Employees with at least 30 years of service and also employees of age 60 or more receive an **extra 3 days**, on top of possible additional days already given;*

3) *If an employee has at least 15 but less than 30 years of service, an **extra 2 days** are given. These 2 days are also provided for employees of age 45 or more. These extra 2 days cannot be combined with an extra 5 days.*

READER. There are so many conditions with various exceptions, that it is difficult to decide what to start with.

AUTHOR. Exactly! And everybody who starts developing a business decision model faces the same issue. Read the problem definition again and tell me how you would describe this problem in one sentence.

READER. Give me a few minutes… OK, I would say that we need to give every employee 22 vacation days and to add possible extra 5, 3, and/or 2 days based on combinations of different factors.

AUTHOR. This is a good summary. I'd add that we need to create a decision model whose ultimate goal is to calculate vacation days.

READER. Yes, it's easy to say, but when I think of how to give an extra 2 days only when an employee has not already received an extra 5 days…

AUTHOR. Don't jump to these details yet. We need a systematic way to develop decision models with much more complex business logic. So, we will follow the OpenRules "Goal-Oriented" approach. Before we start, let's create a new subfolder "VacationDays" inside "openrules.models": it will be as a placeholder for everything our future decision model will need. Let's also create a sub-folder "rules" inside "VacationDays": we will place all our Excel file inside this sub-folder (frequently called "Rules Repository").

Starting with Glossary

AUTHOR. So, our ultimate goal is to calculate vacation days. It's only natural to name the first goal "Vacation Days". OpenRules recommends starting decision model development with the creation of a special table called "Glossary", in which we should describe all our goals, subgoals, and related decision variables.

Let me create the Excel file "Glossary.xls" inside the folder "rules". This file will contain the initial version of our glossary that looks like the following table:

Glossary glossary		
Variable Name	**Business Concept**	**Attribute**
Vacation Days	Employee	vacationDays

Fig. 1-1. Initial Glossary View

The first column of this glossary will contain all decision variables (both input and output) which will participate in our decision model. Our goal "Vacation Days" is an example of an output decision variable which value we intend to calculate. As we go, we will add more decision variables to the Glossary.

The second column contains business concepts, to which our decision variables belong. In this case, we will use only one business concept "Employee".

The third column defines technical names (also called attributes) that will correspond to each variable. We will need them only when we decide to create test cases and to integrate our decision model with an IT system. Just note that contrary to the names of decision variables technical names cannot contain spaces.

READER. But how we will define the business logic for extra days?

AUTHOR. We will specify our business goals using OpenRules decision tables. Let me create the file "rules/Rules.xls" that will contain different decision tables.

Specify Business Goals and Subgoals

The business logic that specifies our ultimate goal "Vacation Days" can be presented in the decision table "CalculateVacationDays", which I created in the first worksheet inside the file "Rules.xls". It is presented in Fig. 1-2:

DecisionTableMultiHit CalculateVacationDays				
If	If	If	Conclusion	
Eligible for Extra 5 Days	Eligible for Extra 3 Days	Eligible for Extra 2 Days	Vacation Days	
			=	22
TRUE			+=	5
	TRUE		+=	3
FALSE		TRUE	+=	2

Fig. 1-2. Specifying the goal "Vacation Days"

This is our first decision table, and I'd like to explain how OpenRules decision tables are organized. Any decision table consists of rows and columns. The first row of a decision table is called the "title row" and describes the decision table type and name. For instance, the type of the above table is defined by the keyword "DecisionTableMultiHit" and its name is defined as "CalculateVacationDays". A table name cannot contain spaces.

I want to bring your attention to a very important convention:

All columns in the first row of any OpenRules table are merged!

The merged cells define the start and end columns of OpenRules tables. The start of any OpenRules table is recognized by a keyword such as "DecisionTable". The bottom of any table is recognized by the last non-empty row. And to be on the safe side, I recommend that you always surround any OpenRules tables by empty rows and columns.

READER. No problem, I will remember this. I see that you use a black background and white foreground in the title row.

AUTHOR. It's just a convention most OpenRules customers make use of for years. In general, you may choose your own colors, fonts, borders, comments, or other presentation elements provided by Excel.

READER. OK. This table looks intuitive enough and I believe I could guess how this table works.

AUTHOR. Good, but as it is our first decision table let me continue to explain its structure. This decision table has 3 condition columns indicated by the keyword "**If**" in the second row, and one conclusion column indicated by the keyword "**Conclusion**". Now, look at the third row. It usually contains the names of the decision variables – one per column.

READER. But contrary to your "If"-columns, the Conclusion-column in this table has two sub-columns and you even merged the name of the variable "Vacation Days" in the third row.

AUTHOR. Yes, this merge is important as well. The first sub-column in the conclusion "Vacation Days" is used for operators such as "=" or "+=", and the second sub-column – for values such as 22 or 5. Starting with the 4th row, we specify our business rules included in the decision table.

READER. Do you have any limits for the number of rules in a decision table?

AUTHOR. Not really, but we should avoid using huge decision table to keep them maintainable. So, as you can see, this decision table contains 4 business rules. The first rule will unconditionally assign 22 days to the variable "Vacation Days" using the operator "=". Then the second rule may add (the increment operator "+=") 5 more days to "Vacation Days" using the operator "+=". But it will occur only if the first condition "Eligible for Extra 5 Days" is TRUE.

READER. So, let me try to explain the third and the remaining rules. The third rule may add 3 more days to "Vacation Days" using the operator "+=", but only if the second condition "Eligible for Extra 3 Days" is TRUE. And finally, the fourth rule will add 2 more days to "Vacation Days" but only if the condition "Eligible for Extra 2 Days" is TRUE and the first condition "Eligible for Extra 5 Days" is FALSE. Aha! This is how we represent the logic *"These extra 2 days cannot be combined with an extra 5 days"* from our problem definition.

AUTHOR. Very good! It's important to notice that our goal "Vacation Days" depends on 3 decision variables (subgoals) which we have introduced:

- Eligible for Extra 5 Days
- Eligible for Extra 3 Days
- Eligible for Extra 2 Days

So, first of all, we need to add these subgoals to our glossary that now will look as in Fig. 1-3:

Glossary glossary		
Variable Name	**Business Concept**	**Attribute**
Vacation Days		vacationDays
Eligible for Extra 5 Days	Employee	eligibleForExtra5Days
Eligible for Extra 3 Days		eligibleForExtra3Days
Eligible for Extra 2 Days		eligibleForExtra2Days

Fig. 1-3. Extending Glossary with new Subgoals

READER. I noticed that you again used Excel's "Merge"-button Merge & Center ▾ to merge all rows in the second column. Did you do it to show that all 4 goals belong to the same concept "Employee"?

AUTHOR. Exactly! Different goals and decision variables should be distributed among the business concepts they belong to.

READER. I got it. But don't we also need to somehow represent the logic of these 3 subgoals?

AUTHOR. Correct. So, let me add another decision table to the file "Rules.xls" (in a separate sheet) to specify the goal "Eligible for Extra 5 Days". Here it is:

DecisionTable SetEligibleForExtra5Days		
If	If	Then
Age in Years	Years of Service	Eligible for Extra 5 Days
< 18		TRUE
>= 60		TRUE
	>= 30	TRUE
		FALSE

Fig. 1-4. Specifying the goal "Eligible for Extra 5 Days"

READER. I believe I know how it works. If "Age in Years" is less than 18, the first rule will set the goal "Eligible for Extra 5 Days" to TRUE. If "Age in Years" is greater than or equal to 60, the second rule will set the goal "Eligible for Extra 5 Days" to TRUE. If "Years in Service" is greater than or equal to 30, the third rule will set the goal "Eligible for Extra 5 Days" to TRUE.

AUTHOR. And if conditions of the first 3 rules fail, the fourth rule will set the goal "Eligible for Extra 5 Days" to FALSE. This is the default rule that covers all remaining combinations of "Age in Years" and "Years of Services".

READER. Wow! It is almost exactly what was expressed in plain English: *"Only employees younger than 18 or at least 60 years, or employees with at least 30 years of service will receive an **extra 5 days**".*

AUTHOR. Or even better, as now you may add more complex extra 5 days eligibility requirements directly to this table.

Single-Hit and Multi-Hit Decision Tables

READER. Why did you use the word "DecisionTable" (at the left top corner) while in the previous table in Fig. 1-2 you used the word "DecisionTableMultiHit"?

AUTHOR. Good catch! The table "CalculateVacationDays" in Fig. 1-2 was a **multi-hit decision table** that executes all satisfied rules. It allowed us to accumulate assigned vacation days by adding extra days when an employee is eligible for them. On the other hand, the table "SetEligibleForExtra5Days" is a **single-hit decision table** that stops the rules execution as soon as it hits the first satisfied rule. Instead of the type "DecisionTable", you may use the equivalent type "DecisionTableSingleHit". What will happen if you make the table in Fig. 1-4 also multi-hit?

READER. I guess the last unconditional rule always will be executed and no employee would ever be eligible for an extra 5 days.

AUTHOR. Very good. What else was different in these two tables?

READER. Your conclusion in Fig. 1-4 does not have a sub-column for as operator and uses the keyword "**Then**" instead of "Conclusion".

AUTHOR. That's right. You still could use a Conclusion-column with two sub-columns, and the first sub-column will always contain the operator "=" or "Is". I just wanted to show you different options. By the way, the keyword "Then" could be replaced with a synonym "Action".

READER. In this table the If-columns use operators and values together, e.g. "<18" or ">=60". Could we use a separate sub-column for the operators similarly to what we did in the Conclusion-column in Fig. 1-2?

AUTHOR. Yes, you can do it as in the following figure:

DecisionTable SetEligibleForExtra5Days		
Condition	If	Then
Age in Years	Years of Service	Eligible for Extra 5 Days
< 18		TRUE
>= 60		TRUE
	>= 30	TRUE
		FALSE

Fig. 1-5. Placing operators in a separate sub-column

Please note the use the keyword "Condition" instead of "If", and that we also merged two sub-columns for "Age in Years". So, it is your decision when to use columns of types If, Condition, Then, Action or Conclusion. There are other types as well, but we will limit ourselves to these for now.

READER. In the table "SetEligibleForExtra5Days" you freely used new terms "Age in Years" and "Years of Service" as the names of conditions. Could we always simply add new terms in plain English?

AUTHOR. Why not? Just make sure that all names are unique and are presented in the Glossary. Do these terms represent new subgoals or are they simply attributes of an employee?

READER. I think they are an employee's attributes and should be considered as input data for our decision model.

AUTHOR. Good. Let me add these decision variables to the glossary as shown in Fig. 1-6.

Glossary glossary		
Variable Name	**Business Concept**	**Attribute**
Vacation Days		vacationDays
Eligible for Extra 5 Days		eligibleForExtra5Days
Eligible for Extra 3 Days	Employee	eligibleForExtra3Days
Eligible for Extra 2 Days		eligibleForExtra2Days
Age in Years		age
Years of Service		service

Fig. 1-6. Adding additional decision variables to the Glossary

And now we should try to specify two remaining subgoals "Eligible for Extra 3 Days" and "Eligible for Extra 2 Days". We may use the table "SetEligibleForExtra5Days" as a prototype.

READER. Could I try to do it myself?

AUTHOR. Of course, I suspect your Excel skills are better than mine. You may copy the worksheet for Extra 5 Days to a new worksheet for Extra 3 Days and create the proper decision table.

READER. I am not sure about this, but I really love Excel and use it a lot. So, our new decision table "SetEligibleForExtra3Days" should implement the following business logic: *"Employees with at least 30 years of service and also employees of age 60 or more, receive an **extra 3 days**, on top of possible additional days already given"*. We can reuse the same conditions and only change the name of the subgoal in the conclusion column. It's easy! Here is my decision table:

DecisionTable SetEligibleForExtra3Days		
If	If	Then
Age in Years	**Years of Service**	**Eligible for Extra 3 Days**
	>= 30	TRUE
>= 60		TRUE
		FALSE

Fig. 1-7. Specifying the goal "Eligible for Extra 3 Days"

AUTHOR. Perfect! I don't think this decision table requires any explanations. Go ahead and implement the last decision table.

READER. OK. Our new decision table "SetEligibleForExtra2Days" should implement the following business logic: *"If an employee has at least 15 but less than 30 years of service, an **extra 2 days** are given. These 2 days are also provided for employees of age 45 or more. These extra 2 days cannot be combined with an extra 5 days"*. I can omit the last statement as we already took care of it when we specified the goal "Vacation Days" in Fig. 1-2. Just one question: how can I say that the "Years of Service" is more or equal to 15 and strictly less than 30?

AUTHOR. Do you remember how you defined integer intervals in school during your math classes? You may write [15..30). The square bracket "[" means that 15 is included and the bracket ")" means that 30 is not included.

READER. Thank you. Now, my new decision table is presented in Fig. 1-8:

DecisionTable SetEligibleForExtra2Days		
If	If	Then
Age in Years	Years of Service	Eligible for Extra 2 Days
	[15..30)	TRUE
>= 45		TRUE
		FALSE

Fig. 1-8. Specifying the goal "Eligible for Extra 2 Days"

AUTHOR. Very nice. This table is self-explanatory as well. By the way, instead of [15..30) you also may write the phrase "more or equal to 15 and strictly less than 30".

READER. In plain English?

AUTHOR. Yes, OpenRules would understand it. However, I believe your interval still looks better. Actually, you may not believe it but we've almost completed our decision model.

READER. That's it? Just a glossary and several decision tables?

AUTHOR. Exactly! From a business logic point of view, the answer is "Yes".

Goal-Oriented Approach to Decision Modeling

AUTHOR. Any decision model in OpenRules is represented by a glossary surrounded by decision tables which specify all goals and subgoals. Our decision model can be viewed as its summary in Fig. 1-9. There are no subgoals left unspecified and it means we have almost completed the development of our decision model.

Such an approach follows the decision modeling practice that we call "Goal-Oriented Approach". We started with a glossary that initially included only one top-level goal "Vacation Days" and one business concept "Employee". Then we specified this goal using a multi-hit decision table in Fig. 1-2. It led us to an introduction of 3 subgoals that determine eligibility for different extra days. Then we specified all subgoals using single-hit decision tables and doing this we kept adding new subgoals and related decision variables to the glossary.

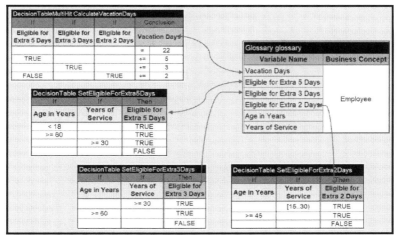

Fig. 1-9. Decision Model: a Glossary surrounded by Decision Tables

READER. I think I understand this approach. But I guess when we build more complex decision models, they will have many more decision tables and probably more complex business logic. They would not fit a diagram like the one in Fig. 1-9.

AUTHOR. You are right, but the diagram is simply of a high-level view of our decision model. We don't need to exactly specify all "arrows" in the diagram because all logical dependencies between different decision tables will be automatically discovered by OpenRules. However, from the decision management perspective, it is very important how you organize and maintain your decision model components (such as decision table and glossaries).

Rules Repository

AUTHOR. For this simple decision model, we created two Excel files "Glossary.xls" and "Rules.xls" in the folder "rules". Real-world decision models can be represented in hundreds or more

Excel files. All together these files comprise a Rule Repository, sometimes also called a "Knowledge Repository".

While OpenRules allows different representations of a <u>Rules Repository</u>, for now, we may consider it as a set of Excel files with various OpenRules tables. These files may be distributed among different folders to cover different business categories and subcategories. Our folder "rules" serves as "Rules Repository" for this simple decision model.

READER. I understand that instead of one file "Rules.xls" we may create multiple Excel files. Can I use xlsx-files along with xls-files?

AUTHOR. Yes, you can. Now to complete our decision model, OpenRules recommends the creation of another file usually called "DecisionModel.xls" in the same rules repository folder "rules". The file "DecisionModel.xls" usually contains two worksheets:

1) The first one includes a plain English description of the business problem similar to the one we used <u>above</u>;

2) The second worksheet contains a special table "**Environment**" that describes the structure of the rules repository.

I've created the file "DecisionModel.xls" with the following table of the type "Environment":

Environment	
	Glossary.xls
include	Rules.xls
	../../openrules.config/DecisionTemplates.xls

Fig. 1-10. Defining the rules repository structure

This table states that our decision model includes the following files defined relative to the main file "DecisionModel.xls":

- Glossary.xls located at the same level as DecisionModel.xls

- Rules.xls located at the same level as DecisionModel.xls

- ../../openrules.config/DecsionTemplates.xls, the standard template file located two levels above DecisionModel.xls in the OpenRules configuration folder "openrules.config".

It corresponds to our current file structure:

- **VacationDays**
  - Rules
    - DecisionModel.xls
    - Glossary.xls
    - Rules.xls
- **openrules.config**
  - DecisionTemplates.xls

In general, an Environment table can include more references to other Excel files or to Java libraries or XML files, but our simple decision model "Vacation Days" does not require anything else.

The file "DecisionModel.xls" will serve as an entry point to our decision model when we decide to integrate it with an IT system.

READER. OK, may I say now that any decision model is comprised of

1) Environment table

2) Glossary table

3) Multiple decision tables for all goals and subgoals?

AUTHOR. This is a good summary. Now I want to point you to one simple but very important capability that helps OpenRules customers to maintain their quite complex rules repository. The decision model "Vacation Days" has only 4 decision tables located in the same file "Rules.xls". What if a decision model contains hundreds or even thousands of decision variables and its decision tables are distributed among different folders, and files, and worksheets? How can they all be managed?

READER. Probably the glossary may help.

AUTHOR. That's right. The glossary shows us all goals and subgoals. But to quickly go from a goal to the table that defines this goal, OpenRules customers frequently utilize Excel hyperlinks to connect goals with the decision tables that specify them.

READER. They probably use Excel's "**Insert Hyperlink**" mechanism to do that – I also use hyperlinks a lot.

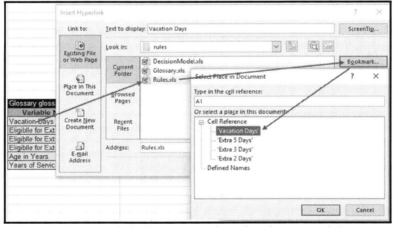

Fig. 1-11. Inserting links between goals in the Glossary and decision tables that specify them

AUTHOR. Yes, and Fig. 1-11 shows how to associate the goal "Vacation Days" inside the Glossary.xls with the table "CalculateVacationDays" defined in the first worksheet of the file "Rules.xls".

READER. I get it: we always should hyperlink all goals in the glossary with the tables that define these goals.

AUTHOR. Yes, it is simple to do but has long-term benefits when you maintain your decision models. Any other questions at this point?

READER. You used different colors and border shapes in the above tables. How important are they?

AUTHOR. They obviously do not affect the semantics and execution logic of those tables. However, it is important to set a certain presentation standard for your organization and to stick to it. For example, as I already mentioned, over the years OpenRules customers use the black background and white foreground in the very first rows of any table. It helps users to immediately recognize what kind of table they are dealing with. The second row in decision tables is usually grey. The use of light blue color for decision table conditions and purple color for conclusion comes from the DMN examples. But again, you may set up your own presentation standard as long as you stick to it.

READER. Got it. So, we may use a goal-oriented approach to create a nice decision model. But how would we know if this decision model will work in the way we expect it to work?

AUTHOR. That's the question that I really wanted to hear! The development of a decision model is not over until we create test cases and run them against the decision model to make sure that the produced results are the same as we expected.

Creating Test Cases

AUTHOR. To test this decision model, we will create test cases in Excel. I will create another file called "Test.xls" inside the folder "rules". This file will contain 3 new tables. First, we need a table that describes our business concept "Employee". It can be done in the following table of the type "Datatype":

Datatype Employee	
String	id
int	vacationDays
boolean	eligibleForExtra5Days
boolean	eligibleForExtra3Days
boolean	eligibleForExtra2Days
int	age
int	service

Fig. 1-12. Specifying a datatype "Employee"

This table starts with the keyword "**Datatype**" following the name of the business concept after a space that usually starts with a capital letter and does not allow spaces inside. The first column contains types of all attributes such as:

- **String** for text attributes
- **int** for integer attributes
- **boolean** for logical attributes
- **double** for real attributes
- **Date** for dates.

The second column contains the names of attributes which should coincide with those which were defined in the third column of the glossary. The very first attribute should have type "String" as it's usually used as an identifier. In this case, we use the attribute "id" of the type String even if our glossary does not use it at all. All other attributes are the same as in the glossary.

After we specify the Datatype table, we may specify many test-objects of this Datatype. The following table specifies an array "employees" that contains 6 test-objects:

Data Employee employees						
id	age	service	eligibleForExtra5Days	eligibleForExtra3Days	eligibleForExtra2Days	vacationDays
ID	Age in Years	Years of Service	Eligible for Extra 5 Days	Eligible for Extra 3 Days	Eligible for Extra 2 Days	Vacation Days
A	17	1	FALSE	FALSE	FALSE	0
B	25	5	FALSE	FALSE	FALSE	0
C	49	30	FALSE	FALSE	FALSE	0
D	49	29	FALSE	FALSE	FALSE	0
E	57	32	FALSE	FALSE	FALSE	0
F	64	42	FALSE	FALSE	FALSE	0

Fig. 1-13. Specifying an array of test-employees

The first row defines the table type "**Data**" following our datatype "Employee" after a space and following the name of the array "employees" after another space. The array name usually starts with a small letter and cannot contain spaces.

The second row lists the names of all attributes as defined in the Datatype table – you can simply copy them and use Excel Paste Special + Transpose to create this row. The third row defines business names of each column that usually coincide with the names of the proper decision variables in the first column of the Glossary (but you actually can use any names here).

The next rows define attribute values for every test-object. For example, the first element of the array "employees" has ID=A, Age in Years=17, and Years of Service=1. All attributes (except those that have type String) should receive some initial values. That's why I set all unknown Boolean decision variables to FALSE and the unknown Vacation Days to 0.

And finally, I create a table of the type "**DecisionTableTest**" that describes test cases with expected results:

DecisionTableTest testCases		
#	ActionUseObject	ActionExpect
Test ID	**Employee**	**Vacation Days**
Test A	:= employees[0]	27
Test B	:= employees[1]	22
Test C	:= employees[2]	29
Test D	:= employees[3]	24
Test E	:= employees[4]	30
Test F	:= employees[5]	30

Fig. 1-14. Specifying test cases with expected results

This table defines 6 test cases using the first column as a Test ID. The second column of the type "**ActionUseObject**" refers to the selected test-objects from the array "employees." Note that "employees[0]" refers to the first element, "employees[1]" refers to the second element, etc. The third column of the type "**ActionExpect**" specifies expected results, e.g. we expect that our first employee "A" should receive 27 vacation days. Can you explain why we expect 27 days here?

READER. The first test-employee is 17-years-old and has only one year of service. So, he is only eligible for the basic 22 days plus an extra 5 days.

AUTHOR. Good. This table may include more columns, e.g. you may add more ActionExpect columns to cover other goals as well.

READER. I cannot help noticing that the preparation of the test cases takes almost as much time as the creation of the decision model itself.

AUTHOR. Yes, and that's how it should be! Many of OpenRules customers maintain a large repository of test cases in parallel with their rules repository. For example, one large international agency uses OpenRules to handle very complex processing logic for legal documents coming from more than 80 different countries. They have country-independent rules and country-specific rules placed in different folders. So, they organize their test cases in a similar hierarchy of folders and whenever they make changes in the rules, they execute all test-cases to make sure that there are no mismatches between expected and actually produced results. I'd recommend that you employ a similar approach when you develop decision models for your organization.

READER. I will remember this advice. And what should we do to execute these test cases?

Building Decision Model

AUTHOR. Before we are ready to execute our decision model, we need to make one more step: **build it**! Don't worry, it is really simple. OpenRules provides a standard batch-file "**build.bat**" that can be found in any OpenRules sample project. I've copied from this file from the project "Hello", pasted it into our project folder "VacationDays", and modified the first line by setting GOAL to our "Vacation Days". Now, this file looks as in Fig. 1-15:

```
set GOAL="Vacation Days"
set INPUT_FILE_NAME=rules/DecisionModel.xls
set OUTPUT_FILE_NAME=rules/Goals.xls
@echo off
cd %~dp0
call ..\openrules.config\projectBuild
```

Fig. 1-15. Building Decision Model

Now I can simply double-click on this file from the Windows Explorer to finalize the model before running it. During this build, OpenRules analyzes the entire decision model starting with the file "rules/DecisionModel.xls" defined as INPUT_FILE_NAME and generates its execution path saving it as a special table in the file "**Goals.xls**". You don't have to even look inside this file, but I don't want to hide anything from you. Here is the automatically generated table of a special type "**Decision**":

Decision DecisionVacationDays
ActionExecute
Decision Tables
SetEligibleForExtra5Days
SetEligibleForExtra3Days
SetEligibleForExtra2Days
CalculateVacationDays

Fig. 1-16. A generated table "Decision" with an execution path

This table contains an execution path inside our decision model that leads to the goal "Vacation Days". It directs OpenRules to execute all decision tables listed in Fig. 1-16 in the top-down order.

READER. But I could create this table manually by myself...

AUTHOR. Yes, you could, and for some complex decision models, it might be the way to go. However, a nice thing about auto-generation of the execution path is the fact that you don't have to worry about the execution order of all your decision tables. Think about real-world decision models that contain hundreds of inter-related decision tables. As I said, you don't even have to look inside this file. Every time when you make some serious changes to your decision model, e.g. adding new goals, you should run "build.bat" to re-generate this file.

READER. OK, I got it. Could we finally execute our decision model?

Executing Test Cases

AUTHOR. We are almost there. To execute our model, we will need to copy from the "Hello" project another standard file "**run.bat**" to our folder "VacationDays" and modified it as shown in Fig. 1-17.

```
set DECISION_NAME=DecisionVacationDays
set FILE_NAME=rules/Test.xls
cd %~dp0
call ..\openrules.config\projectRun
```

Fig. 1-17. Executing Decision Model

It defines DECISION_NAME as "DecisionVacationDays" using the same name as in the title row of the table in Fig. 1-16. It is composed of the word "Decision" and the name of our goal "Vacation Days" with all spaces (and hyphens if any) being omitted. When you double-click on the file "run.bat", you will see the execution results in Fig. 1-18 below.

READER. Wow, it was fast! Let me look at the results more attentively. All 6 test-cases defined in Fig. 1-14 were executed. Very interesting! All results came as expected with one exception: apparently, there is a problem in the third test.

Dialog-Session 1

```
RUN TEST: Test A 2018-08-26 13:19:41.209
   Assign: Eligible for Extra 5 Days  = true
   Assign: Eligible for Extra 3 Days  = false
   Assign: Eligible for Extra 2 Days  = false
   Conclusion: Vacation Days  = 22
   Conclusion: Vacation Days  += 27
Validating results for the test <Test A>
Test A was successful
Executed test Test A in 31 ms

RUN TEST: Test B 2018-08-26 13:19:41.24
   Assign: Eligible for Extra 5 Days  = false
   Assign: Eligible for Extra 3 Days  = false
   Assign: Eligible for Extra 2 Days  = false
   Conclusion: Vacation Days  = 22
Validating results for the test <Test B>
Test B was successful
Executed test Test B in 15 ms

RUN TEST: Test C 2018-08-26 13:19:41.255
   Assign: Eligible for Extra 5 Days  = true
   Assign: Eligible for Extra 3 Days  = true
   Assign: Eligible for Extra 2 Days  = true
   Conclusion: Vacation Days  = 22
   Conclusion: Vacation Days  += 27
   Conclusion: Vacation Days  += 30
Validating results for the test <Test C>
MISMATCH: variable 'Vacation Days' has value '30' while '29' was expected
Test C was unsuccessful
Executed test Test C in 0 ms

RUN TEST: Test D 2018-08-26 13:19:41.255
   Assign: Eligible for Extra 5 Days  = false
   Assign: Eligible for Extra 3 Days  = false
   Assign: Eligible for Extra 2 Days  = true
   Conclusion: Vacation Days  = 22
   Conclusion: Vacation Days  += 24
Validating results for the test <Test D>
Test D was successful
Executed test Test D in 20 ms

RUN TEST: Test E 2018-08-26 13:19:41.275
   Assign: Eligible for Extra 5 Days  = true
   Assign: Eligible for Extra 3 Days  = true
   Assign: Eligible for Extra 2 Days  = true
   Conclusion: Vacation Days  = 22
   Conclusion: Vacation Days  += 27
   Conclusion: Vacation Days  += 30
Validating results for the test <Test E>
Test E was successful
Executed test Test E in 0 ms

RUN TEST: Test F 2018-08-26 13:19:41.275
   Assign: Eligible for Extra 5 Days  = true
   Assign: Eligible for Extra 3 Days  = true
   Assign: Eligible for Extra 2 Days  = true
   Conclusion: Vacation Days  = 22
   Conclusion: Vacation Days  += 27
   Conclusion: Vacation Days  += 30
Validating results for the test <Test F>
Test F was successful
Executed test Test F in 26 ms
1 test(s) out of 6 failed!
```

Fig. 1-18. Execution Results

For the third test-case, OpenRules produced invalid results reported as:

```
MISMATCH: variable 'Vacation Days' has value '30'
while '29' was expected
Test C was unsuccessful
```

AUTHOR. Could you analyze these by looking at the execution protocol? Do we have an error in our business logic?

READER. Let me see. The third employee "C" is 49 years old and has 30 years of service. 30 years of service make him eligible for an extra 5 days. They also make him eligible for an extra 3 days. The Age of 45 years makes him eligible for an extra 2 days as well, but we cannot give him these 2 days as he already received an extra 5 days. So, his total vacation days should be 22+5+3=30 days. But our test case C expects 29 days. This is the reason for the mismatch. Could I change 29 to 30 days in the table "testCases" myself and double-click on "run.bat" again?

AUTHOR. Be my guest.

READER. Great! We don't have any mismatches anymore.

AUTHOR. This was a good teaching moment. Such mistakes could occur when you start building your own decision models. However, you did your analysis based on only a few decision variables. When you have 10 or more decision variables involved in decision making it is much more difficult to explain why certain results were achieved. That's why OpenRules along with the execution protocol such as in Fig. 1-18 also produces the explanation reports in the friendly HTML format.

Explanation Reports

AUTHOR. When you double-clicked on "run.bat" OpenRules also generated 6 HTML-files in the folder "report" (one for each test case). Here is the report "Test C.html" for our third test case:

Decision "DecisionVacationDays" (report/Test C.html)

Executed Decision Tables and Rules (Sun Aug 26 13:19:41 EDT 2018)

Decision Table : Rule#	Executed Rule	Variables and Values
SetEligibleForExtra5Days:3	IF Years of Service >= 30 THEN Eligible for Extra 5 Days = true	Years of Service=30 Eligible for Extra 5 Days=true
SetEligibleForExtra3Days:1	IF Years of Service >= 30 THEN Eligible for Extra 3 Days = true	Years of Service=30 Eligible for Extra 3 Days=true
SetEligibleForExtra2Days:2	IF Age in Years >= 45 THEN Eligible for Extra 2 Days = true	Age in Years=49 Eligible for Extra 2 Days=true
CalculateVacationDays:1	Vacation Days = 22	Vacation Days=22
CalculateVacationDays:2	IF Eligible for Extra 5 Days = true THEN Vacation Days += 5	Eligible for Extra 5 Days=true Vacation Days=27
CalculateVacationDays:3	IF Eligible for Extra 3 Days = true THEN Vacation Days += 3	Eligible for Extra 3 Days=true Vacation Days=30

Fig. 1-19. Explanation Report for Test C

This report shows only those rules which were actually executed in the order they were executed. The first column contains the name of the decision table and the order number of the executed rule within this table. The second column shows the rule formulation collected from all conditions and actions and combined in one statement using the logical connectors IF, AND, THEN. And finally, the third column shows the value of all decision variables involved in this particular rule with their values in the moment of the rule execution.

READER. This is a really helpful report. It actually confirms my analysis. First executed rule was the rule #3 from the table "SetEligibleForExtra5Days". And it set the variable "Eligible for Extra 5 Days" to true. The next two rules similarly set the variables "Eligible for Extra 3 Days" and "Eligible for Extra 2 Days" to true. Then the 1st rule from the table "CalculateVacationDays" assigned basic 22 days to "Vacation Days". Then the 2nd and the 3rd rules from the same table incremented this number with 5 and 3 days, but as we see the 4th rule for extra 2 days was never executed!

AUTHOR. Yes, our users also like these reports as sometimes they explain some really surprising results. We are almost done for today. Let's just summarize the implementation steps we covered today:
1. Create Glossary with a top-level goal
2. Specify the goal using decision tables. It may identify new subgoals and decision variable. Add them to the glossary
3. Specify subgoals using decision tables until there are no unspecified subgoals left
4. Create Test Cases
5. Build the decision model
6. Executed Test Cases
7. Analyze the execution results.

So, today we managed to created and to test our first decision model. Were you able to "touch" it?

READER. I'd say so. I feel now I am ready to implement much more complex decision models. Thank you.

AUTHOR. See you next time.

Suggested Exercises

1. The company decided to give employees who are about to retire an incentive to stay. So, now we should give an extra 4 days to men who are 65 or older and to women who are 60 or older. Copy the folder "VacationDays" to "MyVacationDays" and make the proper changes. Don't forget to expand test cases as well.

2. Replace the rule *"These extra 2 days cannot be combined with an extra 5 days"* with the following constraint *"The total number of vacation days cannot exceed 29 days"*.

Dialog-Session 2: Implementing Decision Model "Credit Card Application"

Discussed Topics:

Related OpenRules Project:
CreditCardApplication

AUTHOR. Today we will develop another relatively simple decision model "Credit Card Application" that also was used as a DMCommunity.org Challenge initially specified by Nick Broom.

Problem Description

AUTHOR. This decision model should analyze a credit card application and based on an applicant's characteristics decide if this application should be accepted or rejected. This problem was derived from a business process described here. There is also a Decision Requirements Diagram that provides a top-level graphical representation of the decision model using the DMN notation. However, instead of analyzing those diagrams, I can simply tell you that the main goal of this decision model is to determine the Application Status that depends on Applicant Demographic Suitability and Applicant Credit Card Eligibility. **The Application Status should be defined as "Accepted" only when Applicant Demographic Suitability is "Suitable" and Applicant Credit Card Eligibility is "Eligible".** There are many rules that describe how to define these suitability and eligibility subgoals and it would be much easier if I describe them to you directly in decision tables. I believe you already have enough information to start the development of our decision model.

READER. I will try as we already know the main goal and its two subgoals.

Starting with Glossary and Main Goal

Just as we did for Vacation Days, first I'll create the project folder "CreditCardApplication", its subfolder "rules", and the Excel file "rules/Glossary.xls". Here is our initial glossary:

Glossary glossary		
Decision Variables	**Business Concept**	**Attribute**
Application Status		applicationStatus
Applicant Demographic Suitability	Application	demographicSuitability
Applicant Credit Card Eligibility		creditCardEligibility

Fig. 2-1. Initial Glossary with top-level goals

AUTHOR. Very good – I see that our previous session was productive. You also may try to specify our main goal "Application Status".

READER. Of course, I can. I will create a decision table "DetermineApplicationStatus" in the file "rules/Rules.xls". Here it goes:

DecisionTable DetermineApplicationStatus		
If	If	Then
Applicant Demographic Suitability	Applicant Credit Card Eligibility	Application Status
Suitable	Eligible	Accepted
		Rejected

Fig. 2-2. Initial Decision Table for the goal "Application Status"

AUTHOR. Looks good. However, to show you more useful modeling capabilities, I'll make several modifications. First, this decision model will have many more rules that we had in the "Vacation Days" model. So, instead of keeping them all in one file "Rules.xls" I suggest creating different rule-files for different goals. So, I renamed your file "Rules.xls" to "ApplicationStatus.xls".

READER. We probably should remember to make the proper changes in our "Environment" table that describes the project's structure.

AUTHOR. This is a good comment – we will do it later. First, let us extend your decision table in Fig. 2-1 to explain why the application was rejected.

Adding Decision Explanations

To do this, I will add one more action using the keyword "**Message**" that will print the reason(s) why an application was rejected. Here is the modified table:

DecisionTable DetermineApplicationStatus			
If	If	Then	Message
Applicant Demographic Suitability	Applicant Credit Card Eligibility	Application Status	Explanations
Suitable	Eligible	Accepted	
Suitable	Ineligible	Rejected	Reason: Applicant Credit Card Eligibility is Ineligible
Unsuitable	Eligible	Rejected	Reason: Applicant Demographic Suitability is Unsuitable
Unsuitable	Ineligible	Rejected	Reasons: 1) Applicant Demographic Suitability is Unsuitable; 2) Applicant Credit Card Eligibility is Ineligible
		Rejected	IMPOSSIBLE: Check for an error in rules

Fig. 2-3. Decision Table "DetermineApplicationStatus" with Explanations

READER. I like such explanations – they probably will be very useful when we create our own decision models. You also changed the borders, but it is not important, right?

AUTHOR. It is not, but it doesn't cost much to do it. What is important is to be consistent even in small presentation details.

READER. What is the reason for the last rule? It would never happen anyway…

AUTHOR. Remember Murphy's law: "If something can go wrong, it will"? We haven't even started to define suitability and eligibility rules, and we cannot be sure we will define them all correctly. It's better to create such an "impossible" trap that may potentially help to explain the unexpected behavior of our decision model in the future.

READER. Thank you, I will try to remember these techniques when I develop my own decision models. Could we continue to specify our subgoals?

Demographic Suitability Rules

AUTHOR. OK, let's start with business logic that defines Applicant Demographic Suitability. Instead of explaining this logic in plain English, I would rather show it to you using a decision table. I placed the following table in the file "rules/DemographicSuitability.xls":

DecisionTable ApplicantDemographicSuitability			
If	If	If	Then
Applicant Years of Age	Application Card Type	Applicant is Existing Customer	Applicant Demographic Suitability
<18			Unsuitable
	Student, Private	FALSE	Unsuitable
	Private	TRUE	Applicant Private Credit Card Demographic Suitability
	Student	TRUE	Applicant Student Credit Card Demographic Suitability
			Suitable

Fig. 2-4. Decision Table for "Applicant Demographic Suitability"

Could you explain this logic?

READER. I will try. First of all, we can see that the goal "Applicant Demographic Suitability" depends on 3 new decision variables: Applicant Years of Age, Application Card Type, and Applicant is Existing Customer. The first rule sets "Applicant Demographic Suitability" to "Unsuitable" if Applicant Years of Age < 18. The second rule does the same if Application Card Type is "Student" or "Private". I don't exactly understand the meaning of "Applicant Private/Student Credit Card Demographic Suitability" in the last column of the rules 3 and 4.

AUTHOR. They are just two other subgoals which we will need to define somehow later. But this table assumes that the calculated values of these subgoals will be used to determine the value of the goal "Applicant Demographic Suitability".

READER. Aha, they are just references and not values like "Suitable" or "Unsuitable". Probably the actual values of these subgoals can be only "Suitable" or "Unsuitable". Correct?

AUTHOR. Correct.

READER. I understand this now, but will OpenRules be able to "understand" this as well?

AUTHOR. You are going to add these two subgoals ("Applicant Private Credit Card Demographic Suitability" and "Applicant Student Credit Card Demographic Suitability") to the Glossary, aren't you?

READER. Of course.

AUTHOR. So, when OpenRules finds that a cell contains the name of a decision variable (or goal) defined in the glossary, it will automatically replace the name with the current value of this variable.

READER. Wow, it's smart! It also makes the decision table like the one in Fig. 2-4 quite intuitive.

AUTHOR. I am glad you like it. Now let's specify the business logic for the goal "Applicant Private Credit Card Demographic Suitability". Fig. 2-5 shows a decision table for this goal. Could you explain its behavior?

Dialog-Session 2

DecisionTable ApplicantPrivateCreditCardDemographicSuitability			
If	If	If	Then
Applicant Sole Annual Income Amount	Existing Customer Outstanding Mortgage Borrowings Amount	Existing Customer Saving and Investments Balance Amount	Applicant Private Credit Card Demographic Suitability
>= 100000			Suitable
	>= 300000		Suitable
		>= 100000	Suitable
< 100000	< 300000	< 100000	Unsuitable

Fig. 2-5. Decision Table for the goal "Applicant Private Credit Card Demographic Suitability"

READER. This decision table uses the long names for decision variables, the meaning of which I may only guess. However, this fact does not make this decision table difficult to understand. As we expected, it defines a value of Applicant Private Credit Card Demographic Suitability as "Suitable" or "Unsuitable" based on different combinations of 3 new factors (decision variables). And there are no new subgoals anymore.

AUTHOR. Why do you think about the 4th rule?

READER. It lists all conditions that are opposite to those defined in the above rules. I think it's fine…

AUTHOR. But is it possible that in some situations no rules from this table will be executed and the goal "Applicant Private Credit Card Demographic Suitability" will remain undefined?

READER. Let me think. This is a single-hit decision table (by default). So, it may reach the 4th rule only when the conditions of the first 3 rules are not satisfied. It means it is impossible that for instance Existing Customer Sole Annual Income Amount < 100000 but Existing Customer Outstanding Mortgage Borrowing

Amount >= 300000. Yes, I believe this table will always work fine!

AUTHOR. And I agree with you. However, would not it be easier just to leave all condition cells in the 4th rule empty? Then "Unsuitable" will become a natural default value for this decision table.

READER. Yes, let's correct it.

AUTHOR. Done. Now please take a look at the decision table in Fig. 2-6 that specifies business logic for the goal "Applicant Student Credit Card Demographic Suitability".

DecisionTable ApplicantStudentCreditCardDemographicSuitability	
If	Then
Existing Customer Current Account Type	Applicant Student Credit Card Demographic Suitability
Student	Suitable
	Unsuitable

Fig. 2-6. Decision Table for the goal "Applicant Student Credit Card Demographic Suitability"

READER. This decision table is really straightforward. Only an existing customer who's the current account type is "Student" is Suitable.

Updating the Glossary

AUTHOR. As we have already introduced a lot of new decision variables, I'd suggest adding them to the Glossary. Keep in mind that some of them belong to the already defined business concept "Application", but others should belong to the Applicant.

READER. I will copy/paste new variables from just added decision tables to the Glossary. Here is my version of the updated glossary:

Glossary glossary		
Decision Variables	**Business Concept**	**Attribute**
Application Status	Application	applicationStatus
Applicant Demographic Suitability		demographicSuitability
Applicant Credit Card Eligibility		creditCardEligibility
Applicant Private Credit Card Demographic Suitability		privateCreditCardDemographicSuitability
Applicant Student Credit Card Demographic Suitability		studentCreditCardDemographicSuitability
Application Card Type		cardType
Applicant Years of Age	Applicant	yearsOfAge
Applicant is Existing Customer		existingCustomer
Applicant Sole Annual Income Amount		soleAnnualIncomeAmount
Existing Customer Outstanding Mortgage Borrowings Amount		existingCustomerOutstandingMortgageBorrowingsAmount
Existing Customer Saving and Investments Balance Amount		existingCustomerSavingAndInvestmentsBalanceAmount
Existing Customer Current Account Type		existingCustomerCurrentAccountType

Fig. 2-7. Updated Glossary

AUTHOR. Good job! So, now we have two business concepts: 1) **Applicant** for decision variables related to a person who applied for a credit card; 2) **Application** for decision variables related only to the application written by the Applicant.

I also want to show you that a table of the type "Glossary" may have one more useful column "Domain" that specifies possible values of different decision variables. Here is my version of the updated glossary:

Dialog-Session 2

Glossary glossary			
Decision Variables	**Business Concept**	**Attribute**	**Domain**
Application Status		applicationStatus	Accepted,Rejected
Applicant Demographic Suitability		demographicSuitability	
Applicant Credit Card Eligibility		creditCardEligibility	
Card Demographic Suitability	**Application**	privateCreditCardDemo graphicSuitability	Suitable, Unsuitable
Card Demographic Suitability		studentCreditCardDem ographicSuitability	Suitable, Unsuitable
Application Card Type		cardType	Student, Private, Standard, Silver, Platinum
Applicant Years of Age		yearsOfAge	
Applicant is Existing Customer		existingCustomer	
Applicant Sole Annual Income Amount		soleAnnualIncome Amount	
Existing Customer Outstanding Mortgage Borrowings Amount	**Applicant**	existingCustomerOuts tandingMortgageBorro wingsAmount	
Existing Customer Saving and Investments Balance Amount		existingCustomerSavin gAndInvestmentsBalan ceAmount	
Existing Customer Current Account Type		existingCustomerCurre ntAccountType	Student, Standard, Silver, Platinum, Black, Balance Transfer

Fig. 2-8. Glossary with Domains Specified

READER. I see. The column "Domain" contains all possible values for some decision variables. I believe it could be very useful.

AUTHOR. It also can be helpful to provide brief descriptions for every decision variable using the cells on the right of each glossary row or just Excel comments (they will be ignored by OpenRules but will help future maintainers of your decision model).

Credit Card Eligibility Rules

AUTHOR. OK, let's define business logic for our subgoal "Applicant Credit Card Eligibility". I placed the following decision table in the file "rules/Eligibility.xls":

DecisionTable ApplicantCreditCardEligibility		
If	If	Then
Application Card Type	Applicant Credit Score	Applicant Credit Card Eligibility
Student	>= 500	Eligible
Student	< 500	Ineligible
Private	>= 750	Eligible
Private	< 750	Ineligible
Balance Transfer	>= 750	Applicant Balance Transfer Credit Card Eligibility
Balance Transfer	< 750	Ineligible
		Eligible

Fig. 2-9. Decision Table for the goal "Applicant Credit Card Eligibility"

READER. This table reminds me of the decision table in Fig. 2-4. It has 7 rules that are supposed to assign "Eligible" or "Ineligible" values to the decision variable "Applicant Credit Card Eligibility" for different combinations of variables "Application Card Type" (already used in table 2-4) and "Application Credit Score" (a new decision variable). The last rule of this single-hit decision table sets the default value "Eligible". Now I am not confused anymore with the use of another decision variable "Applicant Balance Transfer Credit Card Eligibility" on the column "Then". We will add it to the Glossary, and it will be either an attribute of the Applicant or we will have another decision table that will assign one of two values "Eligible" or "Ineligible" to this variable.

AUTHOR. You are absolutely right and here is another decision table that specifies possible values for this new subgoal:

DecisionTable ApplicantBalanceTransferCreditCardEligibility				
If	If	If	If	Then
Applicant Sole Annual Income Amount	Applicant Residential Status	Applicant Application Credit Card Previously Applied in Last 6 months	Applicant Number of Years Address History	Applicant Balance Transfer Credit Card Eligibility
>= 10000	UK Resident	FALSE	>= 3	Eligible
< 10000				Ineligible
	Non-UK Resident			Ineligible
		TRUE		Ineligible
			< 3	Ineligible

Fig. 2-10. Decision Table for the goal "Applicant Balance Transfer Credit Card Eligibility"

READER. I already feel good when you show me such a simple decision table. I only wonder why we need 5 different rules to make this decision variable "Ineligible". Let me replace them with one unconditional rule.

AUTHOR. Not so fast. You are right that in this case, the results will be the same. However, by removing the last 5 rules you will also remove the explicitly expressed business intent of a subject matter expert who oversees this logic. What if this is just an initial version of the decision table and she plans to add more combinations of the Applicant's attributes later? Let's say she decides to make residents of Ireland with Annual Income larger than 30K also Eligible for the balance transfer. We must be careful when we are attempting to make a decision table more compact. That's why usually subject matter experts themselves should oversee all changes to the decision logic.

READER. OK, I will remember this lesson.

Calculating Applicant Credit Score

AUTHOR. To complete the business logic, we only need to specify the decision variable "Applicant Credit Score" used in the table in Fig. 2-9. The proper calculation rules are defined in a decision table in Fig. 2-11.

DecisionTableMultiHit ApplicantCreditScore					
If	If	If	If	Conclusion	
Applicant Number of Default Payments in Last 12 Months	Applicant had declared Bankrupcy	Applicant Years with Current Account Bank	Applicant Amount of Available Credit Used Percentage	Applicant Credit Score	
				=	0
[1--3]					100
[4..6]					50
>6					0
0					250
	TRUE				0
	FALSE				250
		< 1			50
		[1..3]		+=	150
		>3			250
			[0..24]		200
			[25..49]		249
			[50..74]		150
			[75..100]		100
			>100		0

Fig. 2-11. Scorecard for Applicant Credit Score

READER. This is an interesting table. First of all, I noticed that you used the type "DecisionTableMultiHit" in the top-left corner.

AUTHOR. Yes, because this is a typical example of a special type of decision tables called "**Scorecard**". All scorecards usually define a certain score – in our case, it's called "Applicant Credit Score".

READER. I remember the meaning of the multi-hit table: not one but all(!) satisfied rules will be executed. I see that the very first (unconditional) rule will set an initial score to 0. Then all other rules can only increment this score using the operator "+=" that is merged for all possible incrementation rules.

AUTHOR. I like your term "possible incrementation rules". Only those rules that satisfy the conditions for 4 different Applicant's attributes will increment the Applicant Credit Score.

We still should add the newly introduced decision variables to our glossary. By the way, for the Applicant Credit Score you may use the domain "0-999". Make sure that you also linked all goals to the decision tables that specify how to define these goals.

READER. OK. I added new variables to the Applicant and Application business concepts inside our glossary. The finalized Glossary is presented in Fig. 2-12.

Dialog-Session 2

Glossary glossary

Decision Variables	Business Concept	Attribute	Domain
Application Status	Application	applicationStatus	Accepted, Rejected
Applicant Demographic Suitability		demographicSuitability	
Applicant Credit Card Eligibility		creditCardEligibility	
Applicant Private Credit Card Demographic Suitability		privateCreditCardDemographicSuitability	Suitable, Unsuitable
Applicant Student Credit Card Demographic Suitability		studentCreditCardDemographicSuitability	Suitable, Unsuitable
Applicant Balance Transfer Credit Card Eligibility		balanceTransferCreditCardEligibilty	Eligible, Ineligible
Application Card Type		cardType	Student, Private, Standard, Silver, Platinum
Applicant Years of Age	Applicant	yearsOfAge	
Applicant is Existing Customer		existingCustomer	
Applicant Sole Annual Income Amount		soleAnnualIncomeAmount	
Existing Customer Outstanding Mortgage Borrowings Amount		existingCustomerOutstandingMortgageBorrowingsAmount	
Existing Customer Saving and Investments Balance Amount		existingCustomerSavingAndInvestmentsBalanceAmount	
Existing Customer Current Account Type		existingCustomerCurrentAccountType	Student, Standard, Silver, Platinum, Black, Balance Transfer
Applicant Residential Status		residentialStatus	UK Resident, Non-UK Resident
Applicant Application Credit Card Previously Applied in Last 6 months		applicationCreditCardPreviouslyAppliedInLast6Months	
Applicant Number of Years Address History		numberOfYearsAddressHistory	
Applicant Number of Default Payments in Last 12 Months		numberOfDefaultPaymentsInLast12Months	
Applicant had declared Bankrupcy		declaredBankrupcy	
Applicant Years with Current Account Bank		yearsWithCurrentAccountBank	
Applicant Amount of Available Credit Used Percentage		amountOfAvailableCreditUsedPercentage	
Applicant Credit Score		creditScore	0-999

Fig. 2-12. Finalized Glossary

AUTHOR. Looks good. Now, almost all pieces of business logic for this decision model are in place. Once again, we developed our decision model using the goal-oriented approach. We may consider our decision table as a glossary surrounded by decision tables that specify its goals and subgoals:

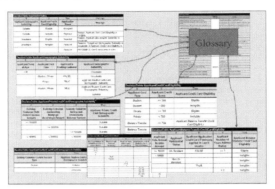

Fig. 2-13. Decision Model as a Glossary surrounded by Decision Tables for Goals and Subgoals

READER. Our Glossary reminds me MS Word Table of Contents: it shows the entire structure of the book with names of all "chapters" (goals) defined in one place. And I can simply click on them to look inside.

AUTHOR. A nice analogy! However, we cannot say that our decision model is completed until we test it. What do we need to test this decision model?

Testing Decision Model

READER. I think we need to do 3 things similarly to how we did it during our <u>first session</u>:

1) Create Datatype tables for Application and Applicant

2) Create Data tables in which we will specify examples of "applications" and "applicants"

3) Create a table of the type "DecisionTableTest" with test-cases and expected results.

AUTHOR. OK. Let's start with Datatype tables.

READER. First, I will create the Datatype table "Application" in the file "rules/Test.xls". I simply copied the Application's attributes from the Glossary and pasted them to the second column, and then I assigned the String to all attributes in the first column – see Fig. 2-13.

Datatype Application	
String	applicant
String	cardType
String	creditCardEligibility
String	balanceTransferCreditCardEligibilty
String	demographicSuitability
String	privateCreditCardDemographicSuitability
String	studentCreditCardDemographicSuitability
String	applicationStatus

Fig. 2-13. Datatype "Application"

Similarly, I created the Datatype table "Applicant" using the Applicant's attributes from our glossary – see Fig. 2-14. In this case, I used the appropriate types like String, int, or boolean based on the possible values of the Applicant's attributes.

Datatype Applicant	
String	name
int	existingCustomerSoleAnnualIncomeAmount
int	existingCustomerOutstandingMortgageBorrowingsAmount
int	existingCustomerSavingAndInvestmentsBalanceAmount
String	existingCustomerCurrentAccountType
int	yearsOfAge
boolean	existingCustomer
int	soleAnnualIncomeAmount
String	residentialStatus
boolean	applicationCreditCardPreviouslyAppliedInLast6Months
int	numberOfYearsAddressHistory
int	numberOfDefaultPaymentsInLast12Months
boolean	declaredBankrupcy
int	yearsWithCurrentAccountBank
int	amountOfAvailableCreditUsedPercentage
int	creditScore

Fig. 2-14. Datatype "Application"

Then I created 4 applications and 4 applicants in the Data tables "applications" and "applicants". Excel's Copy/Paste mechanism really simplified my work: I used the Transpose mode to paste the attributes and decision variable names from our Glossary to the second and third columns of these tables. Here are my 4 test-applications:

Data Application applications							
applicant	cardType	creditCardEligibility	balanceTransferCreditCardEligibilty	demographicSuitabilty	privateCreditCardDemographicSuitability	studentCreditCardDemographicSuitability	applicationStatus
Applicant	Application Card Type	Applicant Credit Card Eligibility	Applicant Balance Transfer Credit Card Eligibilty	Applicant Demographic Suitability	Applicant Private Credit Card Demographic Suitability	Applicant Student Credit Card Demographic Suitability	Application Status
Peter N Johnson	Private	?	?	?	?	?	?
Mary K. Brown	Student	?	?	?	?	?	?
Robert Cooper Jr.	Balance Transfer	?	?	?	?	?	?
Mary K. Green	Balance Transfer	?	?	?	?	?	?

Fig. 2-15. Data table "applications"

Data Applicant applicants

name	existingCustomerSoleAnnualIncomeAmount	existingCustomerOutstandingMortgageBorrowingsAmount	existingCustomerSavingAndInvestmentsBalanceAmount	existingCustomerCurrentAccountType	yearsOfAge	existingCustomer	soleAnnualIncomeAmount	residentialStatus
Applicant Full Name	Existing Customer Sole Annual Income Amount	Existing Customer Outstanding Mortgage Borrowings Amount	Existing Customer Saving and Investments Balance Amount	Existing Customer Current Account Type	Applicant Years of Age	Applicant Is Existing Customer	Applicant Sole Annual Income Amount	Applicant Residential Status
Peter N. Johnson	150000	52000	340000	Standard	45	TRUE	120000	UK Resident
Mary K. Brown	35000	90000	55000	Student	29	TRUE	25000	Non-UK Resident
Robert Cooper Jr.	80000	0	35000	Private	38	FALSE	80000	UK Resident
Mary K. Green	35000	90000	55000	Student	29	TRUE	25000	Non-UK Resident

Fig. 2-16. Data table "applicants" (a partial view)

AUTHOR. OK. And test-cases with expected results?

READER. Here they are:

DecisionTableTest testCases

#	ActionUseObjec	ActionUseObject	ActionExpect	ActionExpect	ActionExpect
Test ID	Applicant	Application	Applicant Demographic Suitability	Applicant Credit Card Eligibility	Application Status
Test 1	:= applicants[0]	:= applications[0]	Suitable	Eligible	Accepted
Test 2	:= applicants[1]	:= applications[1]	Suitable	Eligible	Accepted
Test 3	:= applicants[2]	:= applications[2]	Suitable	Ineligible	Rejected
Test 4	:= applicants[3]	:= applications[3]	Suitable	Ineligible	Rejected

Fig. 2-17. Test-cases with expected results

AUTHOR. Hope you calculated the expected results correctly, but we will know for sure when we execute these test-cases. What else do we need to do to execute them?

Building Decision Model

READER. A few more things. We need to do two more things:

1) Prepare the standard file "DecisionModel.xls" with the Environment table that refers to all our xls-files

2) Build the model to generate its execution path.

AUTHOR. Good. Please copy the old file DecisionModel.xls and adjust its Environment table.

READER. Here it is:

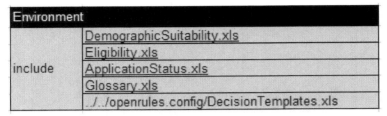

Fig. 2-18. Test-cases with expected results

AUTHOR. Instead of one file "Rules.xls" you correctly included files DemographicSuitability,xls, Eligibility,xls, and ApplicationStatus.xls. I see that you even added hyperlinks to them...

READER. I like Excel's hyperlinks – they really help to navigate through the related documents.

AUTHOR. And now you will use the standard batch-file "**build.bat**" to build the model. Could you adjust this file?

READER. I only needed to change the GOAL. Here it goes:

```
set INPUT_FILE_NAME=rules/DecisionModel.xls
set GOAL="Application Status"
set OUTPUT_FILE_NAME=rules/Goals.xls
set ADDITIONAL_GOALS=true
cd %~dp0
call ..\openrules.config\projectBuild
```

Fig. 2-19. Batch-file "build.bat"

When I double-clicked on this file, it successfully created an execution path in the file "**Goals.xls**". I know that I don't have to look inside this file, but out of curiosity I still want to check which goals and in which order OpenRules plans to execute.

Here is our automatically generated table of the type
"**Decision**":

Decision DecisionApplicationStatus
ActionExecute
Decision Tables
ApplicantPrivateCreditCardDemographicSuitability
ApplicantStudentCreditCardDemographicSuitability
ApplicantDemographicSuitability
ApplicantCreditScore
ApplicantBalanceTransferCreditCardEligibility
ApplicantCreditCardEligibility
DetermineApplicationStatus

Fig. 2-19. A generated table "Decision" with an execution path

Executing Test Cases

READER. We are almost there: I just need to adjust the standard
batch-file "**run.bat**":

```
set DECISION_NAME=DecisionApplicationStatus
set FILE_NAME=rules/Test.xls
cd %~dp0
call ..\openrules.config\projectRun
```

Fig. 2-20. Batch-file "run.bat"

I only needed to modify the variable DECISION_NAME using the
name "DecisionApplicationStatus". It is composed of the word
"Decision" and the name of our goal "Application Status" with
spaces being omitted. And now I will double-click on the file
"run.bat" to execute our decision model against 4 test-cases.
The execution results are shown in Fig. 2-21 (for Test 4 only).

AUTHOR. I can see that you correctly predicted the execution
results.

```
RUN TEST: Test 4 2019-01-07 14:21:47.97
Execute ApplicantPrivateCreditCardDemographicSuitability
  Assign: Applicant Private Credit Card Demographic Suitability = Unsuitable
Execute ApplicantStudentCreditCardDemographicSuitability
  Assign: Applicant Student Credit Card Demographic Suitability = Suitable
Execute ApplicantDemographicSuitability
  Assign: Applicant Demographic Suitability = Suitable
Execute ApplicantCreditScore
  Conclusion: Applicant Credit Score = 0
  Conclusion: Applicant Credit Score += 100
  Conclusion: Applicant Credit Score += 350
  Conclusion: Applicant Credit Score += 600
  Conclusion: Applicant Credit Score += 849
Execute ApplicantBalanceTransferCreditCardEligibility
  Assign: Applicant Balance Transfer Credit Card Eligibility = Ineligible
Execute ApplicantCreditCardEligibility
  Assign: Applicant Credit Card Eligibility = Ineligible
Execute DetermineApplicationStatus
  Assign: Application Status = Rejected
Reason: Applicant Credit Card Eligibility is Ineligible
Validating results for the test <Test 4>
Test 4 was successful
Executed test Test 4 in 31 ms
All 4 tests succeeded!
Executed all tests cases in 117 ms - 2019-01-07 14:21:48.001
```

Fig. 2-21. The execution Results

READER. Yes, I did. Let me also look at the HTML-report for Test 4 to see which rules were actually executed:

Fig. 2-22. Execution Report in HTML (click to enlarge)

You may click on this image to see the entire report. It is interesting that 11 rules were executed for Test 4 – they are shown in Fig. 2-23.

Dialog-Session 2

Decision Table : Rule#
ApplicantPrivateCreditCardDemographicSuitability:4
ApplicantStudentCreditCardDemographicSuitability:1
ApplicantDemographicSuitability:5
ApplicantCreditScore:1
ApplicantCreditScore:2
ApplicantCreditScore:7
ApplicantCreditScore:10
ApplicantCreditScore:12
ApplicantBalanceTransferCreditCardEligibility:3
ApplicantCreditCardEligibility:5
DetermineApplicationStatus:2

Fig. 2-23. The execution rules for Test 4

AUTHOR. Great! We had a productive session today. I recommend you look at the suggested exercises to be ready for the next session. Goodbye!

READER. I will. Thank you - I've learned a lot today. See you next time.

Suggested Exercises

1. Make changes in the scorecard in Fig. 2-11 and re-run our decision model again. You will see how small changes could dramatically change the produced decisions.

2. Add one more test-case to reject the application by two reasons: 1) Applicant Demographic Suitability is Unsuitable; 2) Applicant Credit Card Eligibility is Ineligible

3. Add the rule that allows our decision model to ignore the eligibility rules if the Applicant Sole Annual Income Amount exceeds 90K.

Dialog-Session 3: Implementing Decision Model "Patient Therapy" with Complex Formulas

Discussed Topics:

Related OpenRules Project:

PatientTherapy

AUTHOR. Today we will develop another relatively simple decision model that came from OpenRules decision modeling practice. A large US hospital wanted to build an enterprise-level decision-making system. To compare the competitive capabilities of different business rules products they asked vendors to create a prototype of small medical guidelines which were supposed to help doctors determine patient therapies for different diagnoses.

READER. Sounds interesting but keep in mind that my medical knowledge is very limited.

AUTHOR. I don't know much about medical guidelines either, but remember people who created a chess program that won against the world chess champion were not experts in chess.

Problem Description

AUTHOR. Let's assume that a patient visited a doctor who determined that the patient has Acute Sinusitis. We were asked to implement the hypothetical medication and dosing rules which are presented below exactly as we received them from the hospital.

Medication Rules:

If Patient is 18 years old or older, then a therapy choice is Amoxicillin.

If Patient is younger than 18, a therapy choice is Cefuroxime.

If Patient Penicillin allergic, the therapy of choice is Levofloxacin.

Check if Patient on active medication. Coumadin and levofloxacin can result in reduced effectiveness of Coumadin. Produce the proper warning.

Dosing Rules:

For patients between 15 and 60, the dose is 500mg every 24 hours for 14 days.

If Patient's creatinine level (PCr) > 1.4, commence creatinine clearance (CCr) calculations according to the formula:

$$CCr, \text{ in mL/min} = \frac{(140 - age) \times \text{lean body weight [kg]}}{PCr \text{ [mg/dL]} \times 72}$$

If Patient's creatinine clearance < 50 ml/min, then the dose is 250 mg every 24 hours for 14 days.

Dosing also depends on renal function, immune state, or liver function but the proper rules will be added later.

What is your first impression after reading these rules?

READER. The medication rules do not look any more difficult than our vacation rules which we implemented during our previous session. However, these dosing rules include a rather complicated formula to calculate "something" called Creatinine Clearance (CCr).

AUTHOR. It's good that we will have an opportunity to learn how to implement complex formulas. But I wouldn't worry about this now. As we already know, we should start with an answer to the question: what should our future decision model determine?

READER. I believe it should determine correct medications and their doses for different patients diagnosed with Acute Sinusitis.

Specifying Business Goals

AUTHOR. Good. But to specify the goals for our future decision model, we need to be more specific. The objective of our decision model is to define a patient therapy for the encounter diagnosis of Acute Sinusitis. Such therapy will include the recommended medication and its dose, but it also may produce drug interaction warnings and potentially more information in the future. Based on these considerations let's give the formal names to our main goals and subgoals.

READER. I think we may define this hierarchy of goals:

- **Patient Therapy**
  - **Recommended Medication**
  - **Recommended Dose**
  - **Drug Interaction Warning**

AUTHOR. Very good. The goal names are fixed. In reality, different patient therapies should be defined for different encounter diagnoses, right?

READER. Do you want us to define a decision table that for different encounter diagnoses applies different rules?

AUTHOR. At the very least we should check if the Encounter Diagnosis is Acute Sinusitis before applying the above rules. To move forward, let's create a new decision project "PatientTherapy" with subfolder "rules" which we will use as our rules repository. I suggest we start with the following decision table in the file "rules/Rules.xls":

DecisionTable DeterminePatientTherapy		
Condition		Action
Encounter Diagnosis		Patient Therapy
Is	Acute Sinusitis	"Recommended Medication: " + Recommended Medication + " Recommended Dose: " + Recommended Dose + " Drug Interaction Warning: " + Drug Interaction Warning
Is Not	Acute Sinusitis	Sorry, this decision model can handle only Acute Sinusitis

Fig. 3-1. Determining the high-level goal "Patient Therapy"

READER. Last time you told me that we should always start with creating a glossary...

AUTHOR. That's correct, but it's not clear yet to which business concept the specified goals belong to. So, I decided to jump ahead and imagine how our top-level goal "Patient Therapy" could be defined.

READER. I see, and in this decision table does it. It limits our decision model to the Acute Sinusitis only. If the Encounter Diagnosis is not Acute Sinusitis, our decision model will simply produce the rejection message from the second rule.

AUTHOR. It also defines the main goal "Patient Therapy" using a concatenation formula that combines together Recommended Medication, Recommended Dose, and Drug Interaction Warning.

READER. It looks quite intuitive. I'd even say it is better than plain English. Would OpenRules be able to automatically figure out that our top-level goal "Patient Therapy" depends on subgoals "Recommended Medication", "Recommended Dose", and "Drug Interaction Rules"? Previously subgoals were defined inside the condition columns...

AUTHOR. Yes, OpenRules will figure out these dependencies automatically. Let's start creating our glossary.

READER. No problem. I will create the file "rules/Glossary.xls" and...

AUTHOR. Which business concepts will we use inside the glossary?

READER. Similar to "Employee" in the previous model, we can define the business concept "**Patient**" for whom we need to know age, allergies, weight, and probably more attributes.

AUTHOR. That's correct. But the Patient Therapy belongs not to Patient but rather to a particular doctor's visit. The same is true for Encounter Diagnosis, Recommended Medication and Dose. So, I'd recommend calling this business concept "**DoctorVisit**".

READER. OK, here is the initial version of our glossary:

Glossary glossary		
Decision Variable	**Business Concept**	**Attribute**
Patient Therapy		patientTherapy
Recommended Medication		recommendedMedication
Recommended Dose	DoctorVisit	recommendedDose
Drug Interaction Warning		warning
Encounter Diagnosis		encounterDiagnosis

Fig. 3-2. Initial Glossary

AUTHOR. Very good. I believe now we are ready to start specifying our subgoals. Please start at the medication rules.

Implementing Medication Rules

READER. The first 3 medication rules are:

1) If Patient is 18 years old or older, then the therapy choice is Amoxicillin

2) If Patient is younger than 18, then the therapy choice is Cefuroxime.

3) If Patient is allergic to Penicillin, then the therapy choice is Levofloxacin.

I can easily express the first 2 rules as they depend on Patient's age only. Here is my decision table:

DecisionTable DefineMedication			
Condition		Conclusion	
Patient Age		Recommended Medication	
>=	18	Is	Amoxicillin
<	18	Is	Cefuroxime

Fig. 3-3. Defining Recommended Medication (initial version)

I can add here a second condition to express "If Patient is allergic to Penicillin".

AUTHOR. Not so quick. Of course, you may create a new decision variable "Patient Is Allergic to Penicillin" and check if it is "YES" or "NO". However, do you want to create similar decision variables for all other allergy medications?

READER. Of course, not.

AUTHOR. We also should think about how all allergic medications can be presented in our business concept "Patient". Probably we can get a list of all medications, to which a particular patient is allergic. This list may contain several medications or none. The good news is that OpenRules allows you to use lists or arrays of decision variables by just giving each array a unique name. Then we may use standard operators such as "Include" and "Do not include" with this array. Let me add the proper condition to your decision table. Here it is:

DecisionTable DefineMedication						
Condition		Condition			Conclusion	
Patient Age		Patient Allergies			Recommended Medication	
>=	18	Do not include	Penicillin	Is	Amoxicillin	
<	18	Do not include	Penicillin	Is	Cefuroxime	
		Include	Penicillin	Is	Levofloxacin	

Fig. 3-4. Defining Recommended Medication (second version)

READER. Hmm… I understand why we need to add "Do not include Penicillin" in all previous rules, but I don't like how it looks. What if we change the order of the rules? Look at my version in Fig. 3-5.

DecisionTable DefineMedication						
Condition		Condition			Conclusion	
Patient Age		Patient Allergies			Recommended Medication	
		Include	Penicillin	Is	Levofloxacin	
>=	18			Is	Amoxicillin	
<	18			Is	Cefuroxime	

Fig. 3-5. Defining Recommended Medication (third version)

AUTHOR. Looks better because now we mention Penicillin only once. Will it work? Yes, it will. The reason is that your decision table is "single-hit" by default as discussed during our previous session. Let me remind you what it means. All rules are evaluated in the top-down order. When all conditions of the currently considered rule are satisfied, then the conclusions of this rule will be executed, and all remaining rules will be ignored. Otherwise, the next rule will be evaluated.

READER. So, first it will check if the list "Patient Allergies" includes Penicillin, and if it does, the first rule will select Levofloxacin. If not, it will select Amoxicillin or Cefuroxime based on Patient Age.

AUTHOR. That's right. However, your decision table in Fig. 3-5 depends on the order of rules while the table in Fig. 3-4 does not! It means it can be more difficult to insert new rules in table 3-5.

READER. But table 3-5 looks much simpler and easier to read.

AUTHOR. If you wish, you may merge cells with "Penicillin". However it's hard to formulate a "golden rule" that would tell you which approach is better – it depends on concrete business conditions, such as how many changes do you expect in your decision table. We still may consider completely different approaches, e.g. splitting this table into two separate tables or using a multi-hit table instead of our single-hit tables. We will get back to this problem later on. For now, please choose one of the tables, comment out the other one, and let's move on to dosing rules.

READER. Comment out a decision table? How could I do it?

AUTHOR. You may simply put "//" in front of the keyword "DecisionTable" and this table will be ignored by OpenRules.

READER. OK, I commented out table 3-4. We also need to add another rule to our table. It states that if a patient is taking Coumadin that may interact with Levofloxacin.

AUTHOR. I'd suggest worrying about drug interaction rules later on, probably by creating another decision table. In general, we should never overcomplicate decision tables: it is better to create two different simple decision tables than to have a complex and difficult to understand single decision table. Let's first complete dosing rules, so we can start testing our decision model ASAP.

Implementing Complex Formulas

READER. OK. The dosing rules can be presented using a decision table with three conditions for the patient's age, creatinine level, and creatinine clearance, plus one conclusion that will define the Recommended Dose. I think it is easy enough to do. What really concerns me is the complicated formula that specifies the patient's creatinine clearance as

$$CCr, \text{ in } mL/min = \frac{(140 - age) \times \text{lean body weight [kg]}}{PCr \text{ [mg/dL]} \times 72}$$

AUTHOR. Fortunately, what looks complex is frequently the simplest thing to do. OpenRules allows you to write very complex formulas in a very intuitive way using the DMN FEEL language [1]. Let me show you how to do it the first time and then you will judge if it is complex or "friendly enough". Here is my decision table that calculates the patient's creatinine clearance:

DecisionTable CalculateCreatinineClearance
Action
Patient Creatinine Clearance
(140 - Patient Age) * Patient Weight / (Patient Creatinine Level * 72)

Fig. 3-6. Calculation Formula

READER. Wow! It looks almost exactly as in the specification. You just use the decision variable "Patient Weight" for "lean body weight [kg]" and "Patient Creatinine Level" for "PCr[mg/dL]", correct?

AUTHOR. That's correct! We may assume that these variables are attributes of our business concept "Patient". Please note that DMN FEEL allows us to freely use spaces and even apostrophes inside the variable names, e.g. "Patient Creatinine Level".

READER. Why do we still need to use a decision table to define a formula?

AUTHOR. I can show you an alternative representation:

DecisionTableAssign CalculateCreatinineClearance	
Variable	Value
Patient Creatinine Clearance	(140 - Patient Age) * Patient Weight / (Patient Creatinine Level * 72)

Fig. 3-7. Using DecisionTableAssign

As you can see, this decision table has a new type defined by the keyword "DecisionTableAssign". This kind of table is used when you want to make multiple assignments inside the same table. However, in our case, the standard decision table in Fig. 3-6 is a better choice because if later on, we decide to use different formulas based on liver function, immune state, etc., a regular decision table will be much more flexible than simple assignments.

By the way, instead of the FEEL expression in Fig. 3-6

```
(140 - Patient Age) * Patient Weight / (Patient Creatinine Level * 72)
```

you may also use this Java snippet

```
:= (140 - $I{Patient Age}) * $R{Patient Weight} / ($R{Patient Creatinine Level} * 72)
```

Your programmers may like it, but I suspect you wouldn't.

READER. Of course, I'd prefer to simply write Patient Weight instead of $R{Patient Weight}. Unless it is really necessary. Shouldn't I update our glossary with newly added decision variables?

AUTHOR. Please do it, and don't forget to add hyperlinks for already specified goals.

READER. Here it goes:

Glossary glossary		
Decision Variable	**Business Concept**	**Attribute**
Patient Therapy		patientTherapy
Recommended Medication		recommendedMedication
Recommended Dose	DoctorVisit	recommendedDose
Drug Interaction Warning		warning
Encounter Diagnosis		encounterDiagnosis
Patient Age		age
Patient Weight		weight
Patient Allergies	Patient	allergies
Patient Creatinine Level		creatinineLevel
Patient Creatinine Clearance		creatinineClearance

Fig. 3-8. Updated Glossary

Implementing Dosing Rules

AUTHOR. So, this glossary tells us that it is time to specify the subgoal "Recommended Dose" for which you do not have a hyperlink yet.

READER. OK, I will add a decision table "DefineDosing" by copying/pasting the table "DefineMedication" to another worksheet within the file "Rules.xls". We already have a condition for "Patient Age". Aha! I could again use the interval

[15..60] to check if Patient Age is between 15 and 60 including the bounds.

AUTHOR. You certainly could do that. If you still prefer to use the column of the type "Condition" instead of "If", you use the operator "Within" with a value cell specified as the interval "[15..60]".

READER. No problems. Now I will replace condition "Patient Allergies" with "Patient's Creatinine Level" (as you called it in the formula above). Then I will add another condition for "Patient Creatinine Clearance" and replace the conclusion "Recommended Medication" with "Recommended Dose". My new decision table "DefineDosing" is presented in Fig. 3-9.

DecisionTable DefineDosing						
Condition		Condition		Condition		Conclusion
Patient Age		Patient Creatinine Level		Patient Creatinine Clearance		Recommended Dose
Within	[15..60]					Is	500mg every 24 hours for 14 days
		>	1.4	<	50	Is	250mg every 24 hours for 14 days

Fig. 3-9. Specifying the goal "Recommended Dose"

AUTHOR. Apparently, you are becoming proficient at using decision tables. Your table looks good and it is almost identical to our plain English description.

READER. I like decision tables – they are really intuitive!

AUTHOR. You are right – we frequently understand our rules better when we are trying to represent them in the decision table format. However, I have some questions. What if a patient is older than 60 and has a Creatinine Level less than 1.4 or Creatinine Clearance larger than 50?

READER. Do you mean that I must add rules that cover all possible combinations of Patient Age, Creatinine Level, and Creatinine Clearance?

Decision Table Completeness

AUTHOR. Yes, ideally your decision tables should be "complete" covering all possible situations. However, it is really difficult to satisfy this requirement when you have many conditions. The practical approach is to at least add one more rule for all "otherwise" situations like in Fig. 3-10:

DecisionTable DefineDosing					
Condition		Condition	Condition		Conclusion
Patient Age		Patient Creatinine Level	Patient Creatinine Clearance		Recommended Dose
Within	[15..60]			Is	500mg every 24 hours for 14 days
		> 1.4	< 50	Is	250mg every 24 hours for 14 days
				Is	More dosing rules are needed

Fig. 3-10. The complete decision table for the goal "Recommended Dose"

Now we have the major pieces of the decision logic implemented. So, let's test this initial decision model. Please create test cases.

Creating Test Cases

READER. First, I will create Datatype and Data tables that correspond to our business concepts Patient and DoctorVisit. A quick question. I started to define a Datatype table for Patient, but I don't know what type to use for the attribute "allergies".

AUTHOR. "Patient Allergies" could be presented as a text array, so you may use the type "String[]", where two square brackets "[]" indicates that this is an array.

Using Arrays in Data Tables

READER. OK. Here is my Datatype table for Patient:

Datatype Patient	
String	name
int	age
double	creatinineLevel
double	creatinineClearance
String[]	allergies
double	weight
String	activeMedication

Fig. 3-11. Defining Datatype "Patient"

I added "name" to identify different patients.

AUTHOR. Now you can prepare your Data table with different patients.

READER. Here we go:

Data Patient patients					
name	age	allergies	creatinineLevel	creatinineClearance	weight
Name	**Age**	**Allergies**	**Creatinine Level**	**Creatinine Clearance**	**Weight**
John Smith	58	Penicillin	2.00	0.00	78
Mary Smith	65		1.80	0.00	83
Larry Green	27		1.88	0.00	110

Fig. 3-12. Defining test-patients

AUTHOR. Good. But what if John Smith has multiple allergies, e.g. Penicillin and Streptomycin? In this case, you may split your cell, in which you placed "Penicillin", into two (or more) horizontal sub-rows. See how I did it in Fig. 3-13:

name	age	allergies	creatinineLevel	creatinineClearance	weight
Name	**Age**	**Allergies**	**Creatinine Level**	**Creatinine Clearance**	**Weight**
John Smith	58	Penicillin / Streptomycin	2.00	0.00	78
Mary Smith	65		1.80	0.00	83
Larry Green	27		1.88	0.00	110

Data Patient patients

Fig. 3-13. Defining arrays of allergies

READER. It looks nice and intuitive.

AUTHOR. And it is only natural to do these kinds of changes using Excel or Google Sheets. Now please add data tables for DoctorVisit.

READER. Here is the Datatype DoctorVisit:

Datatype DoctorVisit	
String	encounterDiagnosis
String	recommendedMedication
String	recommendedDose
String	warning
String	patientTherapy

Fig. 3-14. Defining Datatype "DoctorVisit"

And here is test-visits:

Data DoctorVisit visits				
encounterDiagnosis	recommendedMedication	recommendedDose	warning	patientTherapy
Encounter Diagnosis	**Recommended Medication**	**Recommended Dose**	**Drug Interaction Warning**	**Patient Therapy**
Acute Sinusitis	?	?	?	?
Acute Sinusitis	?	?	?	?
Diabetes	?	?	?	?

Fig. 3-15. Defining test-visits

AUTHOR. I see that your added "Diabetes" ...

READER. I want to make sure that our decision model will reject to work with this Encounter Diagnosis.

AUTHOR. Good. Now I believe you can also define the table "testCases" for these three visits. Put only "Recommended Medication" in the expected results and make your best guess.

READER. Here we go:

DecisionTableTest testCases			
#	ActionUseObject	ActionUseObject	ActionExpect
Test ID	**DoctorVisit**	**Patient**	**Recommended Medication**
Test 1	:= visits[0]	:= patients[0]	Levofloxacin
Test 2	:= visits[1]	:= patients[1]	Amoxicillin
Test 3	:= visits[2]	:= patients[2]	

Fig. 3-16. Defining Test Cases

AUTHOR. Don't you expect any results for Test 3?

READER. Nothing because this is an unknown diagnosis.

AUTHOR. Keep in mind that when you leave a cell within the column "ActionExpect" empty, no matching will be checked. OK, do we have everything in place to run these test cases?

READER. Let me check. We should not forget to build our decision model. Here is my the updated file "build.bat":

```
set GOAL="Patient Therapy"
set INPUT_FILE_NAME=rules/DecisionModel.xls
set OUTPUT_FILE_NAME=rules/Goals.xls
cd %~dp0
call ..\openrules.config\projectBuild
```

Fig.3-17. File "build.bat"

When I double-clicked on it, OpenRules successfully generated "Goal.xls". And here is the adjusted file "run.bat":

```
set DECISION_NAME=DecisionPatientTherapy
set FILE_NAME=rules/Test.xls
cd %~dp0
call ..\openrules.config\projectRun
```

Fig. 3-18. File "run.bat"

When I double-clicked on "run.bat", it successfully executed our decision model. The Recommended Medication came as expected in the first 2 test cases. The 3rd test case produces the warning "Sorry, this decision model can handle only Acute Sinusitis".

AUTHOR. Now let's add test cases for Recommended Dose and Patient Creatinine Clearance.

READER. To do this, I need to add two more columns to the table "testCases". I manually calculated the expected Patient Creatinine Clearance. Here is the modified table "testCases":

Dialog-Session 3

DecisionTableTest testCases					
#	ActionUseObject	ActionUseObject	ActionExpect	ActionExpect	ActionExpect
Test ID	DoctorVisit	Patient	Recommended Medication	Patient Creatinine Clearance	Recommended Dose
Test 1	:= visits[0]	:= patients[0]	Levofloxacin	44.42	500mg every 24 hours for 14 days
Test 2	:= visits[1]	:= patients[1]	Amoxicillin	48.03	250mg every 24 hours for 14 days
Test 3	:= visits[2]	:= patients[2]			

Fig. 3-19. Test Cases with more Expected Results Specified

AUTHOR. Let's see what OpenRules will produce this time.

Analyzing Execution Results

READER. We got several mismatches. Here is the execution protocol for Test 1:

```
RUN TEST: Test 1
  Conclusion: Recommended Medication Is Levofloxacin
  Assign: Patient Creatinine Clearance = 44.416666666666664
  Conclusion: Recommended Dose Is 500mg every 24 hours for 14 days
  Assign: Patient Therapy = Recommended Medication: Levofloxacin
  Recommended Dose: 500mg every 24 hours for 14 days Drug Interaction Warning: ?
Validating results for the test <Test 1>
MISMATCH: variable 'Patient Creatinine Clearance' has value '44.416666666666664'
while '44.42' was expected
Test 1 was unsuccessful
```

Fig. 3-20. Execution Results for the First Test Case

Recommended Medication and Dose came as expected. But Patient Creatinine Clearance is not. Wait for a second! The calculated value is 44.416666666666664 while I rounded it to 44.42. Why does it show so many digits after the decimal point?

AUTHOR. This is the default precision when you deal with real numbers. You may ignore this warning, or you can use the produced result as expected.

Formatting Real Numbers using Java Snippets

READER. What if I still want to limit the calculated result to only two digits after the decimal point?

AUTHOR. It would be slightly more difficult. You'd need to switch your calculation formula in Fig. 3-6 to the following OpenRules Java snippet:

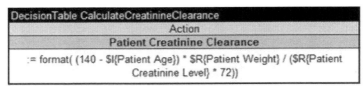

Fig. 3-21. Formatting the Calculation Result to 2 Decimal Points

READER. It is slightly weird, but I did it anyway. Now it really produces

```
Assign: Patient Creatinine Clearance = 44.42
```

All other tests now also have been executed as expected.

AUTHOR. Alternatively, you could add more digits to your expected result and stick to the FEEL formula. Anyway, it shows that you may use Java snippets everywhere instead of FEEL formulas. I can be really useful when you need to invoke standard or 3rd party Java functions such as format(...).

Now it's time to add the required drug interaction rules.

READER. They were formulated as below:

"Check if a patient on active medication. Coumadin and Levofloxacin can result in reduced effectiveness of Coumadin. Produce the proper warning."

I think we just need to add one more variable "Patient Active Medication" and check if it is Coumadin or not.

Implementing Drug Interaction Rules

AUTHOR. I recommend placing this logic in a separate decision table "WarnAboutDrugInteraction" as this logic potentially may become much more complex.

READER. No problem. I added the following decision table to the file "Rules.xls".

DecisionTable WarnAboutDrugInteraction					
Condition		Condition		Action	
Recommended Medication		Patient Active Medication		Drug Interaction Warning	
Is	Levofloxacin	Is	Coumadin	Coumadin and Levofloxacin can result in reduced effectiveness of Coumadin	
				None	

Fig. 3-22. Drug Interaction Rules

I added "NONE" to cover the cases when there are no drug conflicts.

AUTHOR. Good. What else should you do to be able to run these rules?

READER. I've just added the new variable "Patient Active Medication" to the glossary as a part of the business concept

"Patient". We also need to add it to our datatype and data tables for Patient. The modified tables are shown in Fig. 3-23.

AUTHOR. And expected results?

READER. Yes, we need to add another column of the type "ActionExpect" with the title "Drug Interaction Warning" to the table "testCases" in Fig. 3-19. This column is shown separately in Fig. 3-24.

Datatype Patient	
String	name
int	age
double	creatinineLevel
double	creatinineClearance
String[]	allergies
double	weight
String	activeMedication

Data Patient patients						
name	age	allergies	creatinineLevel	creatinineClearance	weight	activeMedication
Name	**Age**	**Allergies**	**Creatinine Level**	**Creatinine Clearance**	**Weight**	**Active Medication**
John Smith	58	Penicillin Streptomycin	2.00	44.42	78	Coumadin
Mary Smith	65		1.80	48.03	83	
Larry Green	27		1.88	0.00	110	

Fig. 3-23. Updated Datatype and Data Tables for Patient

Dialog-Session 3

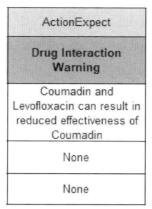

Fig. 3-24. Expected Results for Drug Interaction Warning

AUTHOR. Looks good. Now you need to rebuild and execute the updated decision model.

READER. Yes, I double-clicked on "build.bat" and got no errors. Now I am going to double-click on "run.bat". Here are the results:

```
RUN TEST: Test 1
 Conclusion: Recommended Medication Is Levofloxacin
 Assign: Patient Creatinine Clearance = 44.42
 Conclusion: Recommended Dose Is 500mg every 24 hours for 14 days
 Assign: Drug Interaction Warning = Coumadin and Levofloxacin can result in
reduced effectiveness of Coumadin
 Assign: Patient Therapy = Recommended Medication: Levofloxacin
 Recommended Dose: 500mg every 24 hours for 14 days Drug Interaction Warning:
Coumadin and Levofloxacin can result in reduced effectiveness of Coumadin
Validating results for the test <Test 1>
Test 1 was successful
```

Fig. 3-25. Execution Results for the Updated Decision Model

As expected, now our decision model now also produces the correct Drug Interaction Warnings.

AUTHOR. How about Test 3 with Encounter Diagnosis "Diabetes"?

READER. It did produce the warning "Patient Therapy = Sorry, this decision model can handle only Acute Sinusitis". However, it still calculates other subgoals.

AUTHOR. Because we did not prevent such calculations. As an exercise, you might add an additional condition for "Encounter Diagnosis" to all decision tables. If it was a real project (not just a learning exercise) that supports multiple diagnoses, we would organize our rules repository in a more sophisticated way. Anyway, I think we had a quite productive session today.

READER. Very productive, thank you! I am starting to feel much more comfortable with creating and testing decision models. Only one more question. Will you show me another representation of our table "DefineMedication" for which we created two alternative single-hit decision tables?

AUTHOR. We will do it at the beginning of the next dialog-session when we learn about multi-hit decision tables as well. See you next time.

Suggested Exercises

1. Add more test cases that deal with the problem of incompleteness in our decision tables and analyze the received results.
2. Add a check for the encounter diagnosis "Acute Sinusitis" to the already created decision tables to prevent unnecessary calculation.

Dialog-Session 4: Single-Hit and Multi-Hit Decision Tables

Discussed Topics:

Related OpenRules Project:

AUTHOR. Today we will learn more about different types of decision tables, discuss their execution logic, and when and how better to use them. Decision tables, in general, are known and have been widely used for more than 40 years [10]. There are two major types of decision tables:

- Single-Hit Decision Tables
- Multi-Hit (or Multiple-Hit) Decision Tables

Single-Hit Decision Tables are the simplest and the most popular type of decision tables.

Single-Hit Decision Table Behavior

AUTHOR. As you learned during previous sessions, single-hit decision tables finish their work as soon as at least one rule is executed (its conditions are satisfied) or they may reach their end without satisfying any rule. Such a decision table may hit no more than one rule – that's why we call it "**single-hit**". To identify a single-hit table, along with the keyword "**DecisionTable**" at the left top corner you can use its synonym "**DecisionTableSingleHit**".

READER. During the last session, we created two different representations of the decision table "DefineMedication" in Figures 3-4 and 3-5. I understand that both of them are examples of single-hit decision tables. I still like my table 3-5 more than your 3-4, and you promised to show an alternative representation.

AUTHOR. Yes, and to do this I want to use a multi-hit decision table. I will use my table 3-4 as a prototype and will make only two changes:

1) Replace the keyword "DecisionTable" with "**DecisionTableMultiHit**"
2) Remove values for Patient Allergies from the first two rules.

Here is our first example of a multi-hit decision table:

DecisionTableMultiHit DefineMedication						
Condition		Condition			Conclusion	
Patient Age		Patient Allergies			Recommended	
>=	18			Is	Amoxicillin	
<	18			Is	Cefuroxime	
		Include	Penicillin	Is	Levofloxacin	

Fig. 4-1. Multi-hit Decision Table "DefineMedication"

READER. Wow! Now it looks almost like my table in 4-5: the only difference is that your third rule was the first one in my table 3-5.

Multi-Hit Decision Table Behavior

AUTHOR. Please note that in both cases (3-5 and 4-1) the order of rules inside the tables is important. But more than that, the decision table type "DecisionTableMultiHit" enforces a different behavior:

1) First (before executing any rules!) a multi-hit decision table evaluates all the rule conditions and marks those rules whose conditions are satisfied as "to be executed"

2) Then it executes each of these marked rules in the natural top-down order.

Thus, a multi-hit decision table may execute multiple rules, for which all conditions are satisfied - that's why we call such table "**multi-hit**".

READER. I actually like such behavior. I think the third rule in table 4-1 may **override** the results of a previously executed rule.

AUTHOR. Go back to our decision model "Patient Therapy" and try to execute it using decision table 4-1.

READER. I did and the execution results are the same. However, I noticed that for Test 1 for a 58 years old patient who is allergic to Penicillin, we received not one but two(!) conclusions:

```
Decision DeterminePatientTherapy: Define
Medication
Conclusion: Recommended Medication Is Amoxicillin
[Amoxicillin]
Conclusion: Recommended Medication Is Levofloxacin
[Levofloxacin]
```

Fig. 4-2. Example of rule overrides

It means that our first rule recommended Amoxicillin. The second rule was omitted as our patient is older than 18. And finally, our third rule that does not care about Age, decided to replace the recommended medication with Levofloxacin!

AUTHOR. That's exactly what we wanted, and it is very similar to the initial <u>specification</u> in plain English.

READER. I think it is the best representation so far!

Which Decision Table Type is Better?

AUTHOR. I don't want you to be overly optimistic. As I already mentioned, there is no "golden" rule for which type of decision table is the best – it really depends on your particular case: how many rules this table has, how it's going to be modified in the future, etc. It would be much more productive if you are simply aware of different available options and gain experience applying them in various situations. So, let's consider more examples.

READER. I love to learn by examples.

Back to Vacation Days Example

AUTHOR. Let's go back to our first decision model "Vacation Days". Our model used 4 decision tables: one multi-hit (Fig. 1-2) and 3 single-hit (Fig. 1-4, 1-5, and 1-7). It is possible to implement the entire decision model using only one decision table. Not that I'd recommend this approach in practice, but it may be useful as a learning exercise. So, here is an implementation that uses a single-hit decision table:

DecisionTable DefineVacationDays		
If	If	Then
Age in Years	Years of Service	Vacation Days
<18		22 + 5
[18..45)	<15	22
[18..45)	[15..30)	22 + 2
[18..45)	>=30	22 + 5 + 3
[45..60)	<15	22 + 2
[45..60)	[15..30)	22 + 2
[45..60)	>=30	22 + 5 + 3
60+		22 + 5 +3

Fig. 4-3. Decision model "Vacation Days" implemented as one single-hit decision table

READER. I like this implementation – just one decision table that looks similar to what was described in plain English.

AUTHOR. This table will produce the same results and it is much more compact in comparison with the decision model created during our first sessions. However, this implementation has at least two serious drawbacks:

1) It hides the business logic, e.g. how can you extract from this table the rules *"These extra 2 days cannot be combined with an extra 5 days"*?

2) Would you be able to add new rules to this table?

I certainly prefer our initial decision model as more explicit and much more flexible to changes.

READER. I must agree with you.

AUTHOR. Still, let's look closer at this single-hit decision table. Even if you change the rules order inside the table, it will continue to work. The reason for this is the fact that all the rules inside this table are mutually-exclusive! What will happen if we replace the type of this table with "DecisionTableMultiHit"?

READER. Let me think... Actually, it should produce the same results.

AUTHOR. Yes, thanks to the fact that all the rules are mutually exclusive.

READER. I see. So, wouldn't you recommend always making rules inside a decision table mutually-exclusive? Probably this could be our "golden" rule...

Can We Make All Rules Mutually-Exclusive?

AUTHOR. Unfortunately, it's wishful thinking. In this particular case, for only two decision variables we created 8 different combinations (rules). Let's assume that the company decides to change its vacation policy and give different vacation days to people who worked for less than 5, 10, and 15 years.

READER. In this case, we will need to add more rules with new conditions in the second column...

AUTHOR. And the number of rules will grow quickly. Now, think about what will happen if we also need to consider additional factors, e.g. Work Type, Gender, etc. When the number of variables inside a decision table grows just a little bit (mathematicians call it "logarithmically") the number of their possible combinations grows really fast ("exponentially"). Unfortunately, many real-world decision tables have hundreds or even thousands of rules and some of them depend on each other.

READER. Yep. I believe I myself could give you a few examples of such large decision tables from my own business domain.

AUTHOR. Don't get me wrong: it is a very good practice to try to cover ALL possible combinations of decision variables by making your decision table **complete** with all rules being mutually-exclusive. Do it whenever you can!

More than that, experienced decision modelers recommend splitting large decision tables into multiple smaller tables, which may follow this "golden" rule - see for example the design pattern "Divide and Conquer" in [6] that sometimes is also called "Separation of Concerns". Unfortunately, it is not always possible, and we have to consider other methods to minimize the total number of rules in our decision tables.

Now I want to use the same "VacationDays" problem to show you some advantages of multi-hit decision tables. There is a minor thing that annoys me in the above single-hit decision table in Fig. 4-3: the number 22 (basic vacation days) is repeated inside every rule!

READER. It slightly annoyed me too but...

AUTHOR. Here is how it to avoid this using a multi-hit decision table:

DecisionTableMultiHit DefineVacationDays			
Condition	Condition	Conclusion	
Age in Years	**Years of Service**	**Vacation Days**	
		=	22
<18		+=	5
>=18	>=30	+=	5
>=60	<30	+=	5
	>=30	+=	3
>=60	<30	+=	3
[45..60)	<30	+=	2
<45	[15..30)	+=	2

Fig. 4-4. Decision model "Vacation Days" implemented as one multi-hit decision table

READER. Wow! You just give everybody 22 days unconditionally at the very first rule and then the remaining rules may add extra days on an as needed basis.

AUTHOR. Exactly! Does this table remind you something that we've already done previously?

READER. Wait for a second: this is a scorecard! It is very similar to the scorecard we used in the decision model "Credit Card Application" to calculate Applicant Credit Score.

AUTHOR. Yes, the variable "Vacation Days" can be considered as a "score" that simply accumulates days. Which decision table do you like more 4-3 or 4-4?

READER. The table 4-4 defines 22 days only once and extra days are more clearly defined. However, we didn't win in the total number of rules - both tables have 8 rules.

AUTHOR. That's true: there are always pros and cons. For example, it's not immediately clear if table 4-4 covers all intervals or if it leaves some gaps. So, as I said, our initial approach is certainly preferable than both decision tables 4-3 and 4-4.

AUTHOR. Now I want to talk about the default values. Where did we put the default (or initial) values in single-hit and in multi-hit decision tables?

Default Values in Decision Tables

READER. In all our single-hit decision tables we put the default value in the last unconditional rule. It will use this value only when all other rules in a single-hit table fail.

AUTHOR. Correct. Let's formulate the common recommendation:

*"If you use a **single-hit** decision table, always put the default value in the very **last** rule."*

How about multi-hit decision tables?

READER. Based on the multi-hit tables we used so far, I believe the default value should be defined by the very first rule.

AUTHOR. Correct again. Let's formulate another common recommendation:

*"If you use a **multi-hit** decision table, always put the default value in the very **first** rule."*

READER. Should not we also say that such "default" rules are also unconditional?

AUTHOR. Frequently, but not always. Sometimes the default value can depend on other conditions. There could be not one but several rules that set default values at the end of a single-hit decision table or at the beginning of a multi-hit table.

READER. I think now I have a much better understanding of when to use single-hit and multi-hit decision tables.

AUTHOR. No more questions?

READER. To tell you the truth, I don't completely understand why is it important that a multi-hit table evaluates the rule conditions before executing the rules? We could just say that a multi-hit decision table executes all satisfied rules in top-down order...

Why Multi-Hit Table Evaluates Rule Conditions Before Executing The Rules

AUTHOR. I am glad you asked this question. Many people even among experienced decision modelers have a similar misconception. We really need to clarify the way in which multi-hit tables are being executed. It's always better to do it using an example.

Let's consider almost a trivial example. Let's assume that you need to create a decision table called "Swap" that does the following:

```
If X is equal to 1 make it 2.
If X is equal to 2 make it 1.
```

READER. It is trivial. Here is my decision table:

DecisionTable Swap	
If	Then
X	X
1	2
2	1

Fig. 4-5. Single-Hit Decision Table "Swap Two Numbers"

AUTHOR. Yes, for this single-hit table everything is clear: only the first **or** the second rule will be executed. But what if we make this table multi-hit as below?

DecisionTableMultiHit Swap	
If	Then
X	X
1	2
2	1

Fig. 4-6. Multi-Hit Decision Table "Swap Two Numbers"

READER. Let me analyze its behavior. Let's say that initially, X is equal to 1. Then the first rule will be executed and X will become 2. Then the second rule should also be executed as X is equal 2, and X will become 1 again. So, this multi-hit table will not work!

AUTHOR. You are wrong, and the reason is exactly the first point of the <u>multi-hit table behavior</u>. Let me repeat it again:

1) First (before executing any rules!) a multi-hit decision table evaluates all the rule conditions and marks those rules whose conditions are satisfied as "to be executed"

2) Then it executes each of these marked rules in the natural top-down order.

So, at the very beginning only the first rule will be marked as "to be executed", and independent of the first rule execution the second one will not be marked for execution. And if X is equal to 2, then only the second rule will be evaluated as "to be executed" and then it will be really executed by assigning the value 1 to X. Thus, both single-hit and multi-hit tables will produce the correct results!

READER. Wow, now I believe I understand WHY a multi-hit table evaluates all rule conditions before executing the rules.

AUTHOR. Great! Let's discuss another important observation about decision tables.

How to Use Logical "AND" and "OR" in Decision Tables

It is very important to stress that

"All conditions are connected by the logical AND"

For example, when we read the 4th rule in the decision table in Fig. 4-4 we say:

> "**IF** *Age in Years* >= *60* **AND** *Years In Service* < *30*
> **THEN** *Increment Vacation Days by 5*"

Decision tables do not use the logical connector OR.

READER. I understand this. However, we actually use OR when we add additional rules to the same decision table.

AUTHOR. That's correct, and this is also an important common convention for decision tables. Please note that a decision table may contain several actions (conclusions) but they also are connected by the logical AND.

READER. Still, what if I need to express the following rule:

*"If Employment Status Is Unemployed **OR** Retired Then do something"*?

Should I create separate rules for Unemployed, Retired, and possibly many more values of the Employment Status?

Comma as an OR-operator Inside Lists of Values

AUTHOR. Of course, not! You can simply use one condition with the operator "Is One Of" and all possible values like "Unemployed, Retired" listed inside the same cell separated by commas. For example, look at the decision table used in one of OpenRules sample decision models called "Loan Pre-Qualification" presented in Fig. 4-7.

DecisionTableMultiHit DetermineDebtResearchResult						
If	If	If	If	If	Condition	Then
Mort gage Holder	Outside Credit Score	Loan Holder	Credit Card Balance	Education Loan Balance	Internal Credit Rating	Debt Research Result
Yes						High
No	(100..550]					High
No	(550..900]	Yes	<=0			Mid
No	(550..900]	Yes	>0	>0		High
No	(550..900]	Yes	>0	<=0	Is One Of A, B, C	High
No	(550..900]	Yes	>0	<=0	Is One Of D, F	Mid
No	(550..900]	No	>0			Low
No	(550..900]	No	<=0	<=0		Low
No	(550..900]	No	<=0	>0	Is One Of D, F	High
No	(550..900]	No	<=0	>0	Is One Of A, B, C	Low

Fig. 4-7. Using a comma as "OR" within a list of values

This table uses the operator "Is One Of" to define different conditions for "Internal Credit Rating" with lists of values such as "A, B, C". This condition will be satisfied if the actual value of the variable "Internal Credit Rating" is "A" or "B" or "C".

READER. It looks quite intuitive and readable to me. Just one quick question: what if a value in the list already contains a comma?

AUTHOR. In this case, instead of a comma, you may specify another separator, e.g. "^". All you need to do is to add this separator at the end of your operator, e.g. instead of "Is One Of" you can write "Is One Of separated by ^".

I believe now you are ready to solve one of the challenges published by DMCommunity.org that uses these features.

Decision Model "Up-Selling Rules"

This challenge is called "Up-Selling Rules" and is described at https://dmcommunity.org/challenge/challenge-april-2018.
Imagine that your company wants to offer its customers new products following these up-sell rules:

Customer Profile		Customer Products		Customer Products		Offered Products		Recommendation
Is One Of	Bronze,Silver	Include	Product 1	Do Not Include	Product 2	Are	Product 2, Product 4, Product 5	Additional Products 2,4,5
Is One Of	Bronze,Silver	Include	Product 1, Product 3	Do Not Include	Product 6, Product 7, Product 8	Are	Product 6, Product 7, Product 8	Additional Products 6,7,8
Is One Of	Bronze,Silver	Include	Product 1, Product 2	Do Not Include	Product 6, Product 7, Product 8	Are	Product 4, Product 5, Product 7, Product 8, Product 9	Additional Products 4,5,7,8,9
Is One Of	Gold	Include	Product 1	Do Not Include	Product 6, Product 7, Product 5	Are	Product 9, Product 7, Product 8, Product 4, Product 5, Product 10	Gold Package
Is One Of	Platinum	Include	Product 1, Product 2	Do Not Include	Product 6, Product 7, Product 5	Are	Product 9, Product 7, Product 8 with no annual fee, Product 4, Product 5 with no charge, Product 10	Platinum Package

Fig. 4-8. Product Up-Sell Rules

The first condition uses different customer profiles defined in this table:

Combined Balance	Customer Profile
[500..2000)	Bronze
[2000..5000)	Silver
[5000..15000)	Gold
>= 15000	Platinum

Dialog-Session 4

Fig. 4-9. Customer Profiling Rules

The second condition checks the products that a customer already has, and the third condition checks the products that a customer does not have yet. The first action offers a customer some additional products and the second action produces a comment that specifies the offered package (if any).

READER. You want me to build the proper decision model now?

AUTHOR. Why not? You already have enough knowledge to do it and if necessary, I am here to help. So, go ahead with our goal-oriented approach.

READER. OK, let's do it. I start with the question "what is the goal of our decision model?" Probably it is a list of products we want to offer to our customer.

AUTHOR. Very good. The table 4-8 already provides us with the name for this goal: "**Offered Products**". Before you start creating new files and tables, I suggest in this simple case to use only one file "DecisionUpSell.xls", in which you can put all tables which we usually keep in separate files for Rules, Glossary, and DecisionModel.

READER. OK, my first table in this file will be the Glossary:

Glossary glossary		
Variable Name	**Business Concept**	**Attribute**
Offered Products	Customer	offeredProducts

Fig. 4-10. Initial Glossary with the goal "Offered Products"

AUTHOR. Keep going. Now I want to start with the table in Fig. 4-9 that looks to me like a very simple single-hit decision table. Here it is in the OpenRules format:

DecisionTable DefineCustomerProfile	
If	Then
Combined Balance	Customer Profile
[500..2000)	Bronze
[2000..5000)	Silver
[5000..15000)	Gold
>= 15000	Platinum

Fig. 4-11. Decision Table "DefineCustomerProfile"

AUTHOR. Yes, it is simple. But what if Combined Balance < 500? They don't mention this case, but we should think about all possible situations.

READER. OK, I can add one more rule at the end with some default value, e.g. UNKNOWN.

AUTHOR. To make this simple table complete, it's more natural just to add one more rule for Combined Balance < 500 and call the profile "New".

READER. I will put this rule at the very beginning and all possible cases will be covered. Here we go:

DecisionTable DefineCustomerProfile	
If	Then
Combined Balance	Customer Profile
< 500	New
[500..2000)	Bronze
[2000..5000)	Silver
[5000..15000)	Gold
>= 15000	Platinum

Fig. 4-12. Decision Table "DefineCustomerProfile" (complete)

AUTHOR. Good, this table is complete. How about the table with up-selling rules?

READER. I know that I can use the operator "Is One of" with possible values like "Bronze, Silver". But I am not sure about other operators such as "Include", "Do Not Include", and "Are".

AUTHOR. This list of operators supported by OpenRules can be found in **OpenRules** <u>User Manual</u> on pages 23-25. In particular, OpenRules supports operators:

- **Include** with a synonym "Include All"
- **Exclude** with synonyms "Exclude One Of", "Do Not Include", "Does Not Include", "Include Not All"
- **Are** that adds one or more values listed through comma to a conclusion variable that is assumed to be an array or a list.

So, you can use them exactly as they are defined in Fig. 4-8.

READER. Great! In this case I can easily convert this table to the OpenRules format – see Fig. 4-14.

AUTHOR. I can see that you added the default rule at the end of this single-hit table. This is a smart addition.

READER. Thanks. To insert a comment, I could use the column of the type "Message" as we did during our second session in <u>Fig. 2-3</u>. But what if we want to return the produced comments to the system that will use our decision table? So, I decided to add one more decision variable "Recommendation" in the column of the standard type "Action". I also added more comments to every rule.

DecisionTable DefineUpSellProducts								
Condition		Condition		Condition		Conclusion		Action
Customer Profile		Customer Products		Customer Products		Offered Products		Recommendation
Is One Of	Bronze,Silver	Include	Product 1	Do Not Include	Product 2	Are	Product 2, Product 4, Product 5	Additional Products 2,4,5
Is One Of	Bronze,Silver	Include	Product 1, Product 3	Do Not Include	Product 6, Product 7, Product 8	Are	Product 6, Product 7, Product 8	Additional Products 6,7,8
Is One Of	Bronze,Silver	Include	Product 1, Product 2	Do Not Include	Product 6, Product 7, Product 8	Are	Product 4, Product 5, Product 7, Product 8, Product 9	Additional Products 4,5,7,8,9
Is One Of	Gold	Include	Product 1	Do Not Include	Product 6, Product 7, Product 5	Are	Product 9, Product 7, Product 8, Product 4, Product 5, Product 10	Gold Package
Is One Of	Platinum	Include	Product 1, Product 2	Do Not Include	Product 6, Product 7, Product 5	Are	Product 9, Product 7, Product 8 with no annual fee, Product 4, Product 5 with no charge, Product 10	Platinum Package
						Are	None	Sorry, no products to offer

Fig. 4-14. Decision Table "DefineUpSellProducts"

AUTHOR. I like what you are doing. Now you only need to add new decision variables to the glossary and start testing.

READER. Here is the updated glossary:

Glossary glossary		
Variable Name	**Business Concept**	**Attribute**
Offered Products		offeredProducts
Customer Profile		profile
Combined Balance	Customer	combinedBalance
Customer Products		existingProducts
Recommendation		recommendation

Fig. 4-15. Updated Glossary

Now, our decision logic is completed, and I can build our decision model.

AUTHOR. Go ahead.

READER. As we use only one file "DecisionUpSell.xls" we don't need "DecisionModel.xls". So, I will simply adjust the batch file "build.bat" as in Fig. 4-16.:

```
set INPUT_FILE_NAME=rules/DecisionUpSell.xls
set GOAL="Offered Products"
set OUTPUT_FILE_NAME=rules/Goals.xls
cd %~dp0
call ..\openrules.config\projectBuild
```

Fig.4-16. File "build.bat"

To build the decision model, I double-clicked on this file... OOPS, I got many strange looking errors:

```
INITIALIZE OPENRULES ENGINE 7.0.0 Evaluation Version (build 11182018) fo
Exception in thread "main"     at file:rules/DecisionUpSell.xls?sheet=Gl
    at file:rules/DecisionUpSell.xls?sheet=CustomerProfileRules&range=B2
    at file:rules/DecisionUpSell.xls?sheet=UpSellRules&range=B2:J10&open
org.openl.syntax.SyntaxErrorException: Error: Template GlossaryTemplate
java.lang.RuntimeException: Template GlossaryTemplate could not be found
```

Fig.4-17. Errors caused by missing Environment table

AUTHOR. The actual error says:

Template GlossaryTemplate could not be found

The reason for this error is the fact that along with the file "DecisionModel.xls" you've thrown away the table Environment that refers to the standard OpenRules templates including "GlossaryTemplate". You need to add the table "Environment" to your file "DecisionUpSell.xls" even if refers only to the standard file "../../openrules.config/DecisionTemplates.xls"

READER. OK, I added the following table:

Environment	
include	../../openrules.config/DecisionTemplates.xls

Fig.4-18. The Environment table

Now OpenRules has successfully built our model and generated the file "Goals.xls".

AUTHOR. Good. Let's quickly add Datatype, Data, and DecisionTableTest tables to make sure that our decision model works as expected. You still need to put all testing tables into a separate file "Test.xls".

READER. OK. Here is my Datatype table "Customer":

Datatype Customer	
String	name
String[]	existingProducts
int	combinedBalance
String	profile
String	recommendation
String[]	offeredProducts

Fig. 4-19. Datatype table "Customers"

AUTHOR. You correctly used String[] to indicate that "existingProducts" and "offered" are arrays of strings. Now, when you create a Data table for customers, you may create sub-columns to define "Existing Products".

READER. Like in Fig. 4-20?

Data Customer customers						
name	existingProducts			combinedBalance	profile	recommendation	offeredProducts
Name	Existing Products			Combined Balance	Profile	Recommendation	Offered Products
John	Product 1	Product 2	Product 3	$4,500.00	?	?	?
Larry	Product 1	Product 5		$7,000.00	?	?	?
Mary	Product 1	Product 2		$17,000.00	?	?	?

Fig. 4-20. File "run.bat"

AUTHOR. Exactly. By the way, instead of sub-columns, you may use sub-rows as well but, in this case, you would need to merge other cells for the same customer. So, you defined 3 test-customers. Where are your expected results?

READER. In the following table "testCases" in Fig. 4-21:

DecisionTableTest testCases		
#	ActionUseObject	ActionExpect
Test ID	**Customer**	**Recommendation**
John	:= customers[0]	Additional Products 6,7,8
Larry	:= customers[1]	Gold Package
Mary	:= customers[2]	Platinum Package

Fig. 4-21. File "run.bat"

AUTHOR. Looks good. Let's check it your expectations are right.

READER. First, I will adjust the batch-file "run.bat":
it, OpenRules successfully generated "Goal.xls". And here is the adjusted file "run.bat":

```
set DECISION_NAME=DecisionOfferedProducts
set FILE_NAME=rules/Test.xls
cd %~dp0
call ..\openrules.config\projectRun
```

Fig. 4-22. File "run.bat"

And the execution results are presented in Fig. 4-23.

AUTHOR. I can see that "All 3 tests succeeded!". Congratulation: Today you did manage to build a good decision model for the DMCommunity Challenge.

READER. I feel quite comfortable with building such decision models now. I'm looking forward to learning more advanced decision modeling concepts.

AUTHOR. See you at the next session.

```
RUN TEST: John 2019-01-10 18:59:00.946
Execute DefineCustomerProfile
  Conclusion: Customer Profile Is Silver
Execute DefineUpSellProducts
  Conclusion: Offered Products Are Offered Products
  Assign: Recommendation = Additional Products 6,7,8
Validating results for the test <John>
John was successful
Executed test John in 16 ms

RUN TEST: Larry 2019-01-10 18:59:00.962
Execute DefineCustomerProfile
  Conclusion: Customer Profile Is Gold
Execute DefineUpSellProducts
  Conclusion: Offered Products Are Offered Products
  Assign: Recommendation = Gold Package
Validating results for the test <Larry>
Larry was successful
Executed test Larry in 0 ms

RUN TEST: Mary 2019-01-10 18:59:00.962
Execute DefineCustomerProfile
  Conclusion: Customer Profile Is Platinum
Execute DefineUpSellProducts
  Conclusion: Offered Products Are Offered Products
  Assign: Recommendation = Platinum Package
Validating results for the test <Mary>
Mary was successful
Executed test Mary in 15 ms
All 3 tests succeeded!
```

Fig. 4-23. File "run.bat"

Suggested Exercises

Analyze and execute the decision model "LoanPreQualification". Modify it by changing the decision table "DetermineDebtResearchResults" to become single-hit instead of multi-hit and explain why the results are different.

Dialog-Session 5: Dealing with Collections of Objects and Iterations

Discussed Topics:

Related OpenRules Project:

AUTHOR. We've already covered the most frequently used decision modeling concepts including decision variables, glossaries, and various decision tables. So far, we have considered separate business concepts (objects) and business rules defined using their attributes. You've seen examples where decision variables themselves were arrays as in our decision model "Up-Selling Rules". In real-world applications, your decision models frequently have to deal with collections of objects such as customers, patients, accounts, etc. Today I want to show you how decision models can make a decision by processing an array (list) of objects.

Collections of Objects

Let's say your company wants to determine the minimal or maximal salaries of employees in different departments. It means you need somehow to **iterate through an array** of employees and check certain conditions against each employee.

Usually, in such situations, programmers use different types of loops. For example, in Java you can calculate a maximal salary by writing something like this:

```
int maxSalary = 0;
for(Employee employee : employees) {
    if (employee.salary > maxSalary)
        maxSalary = employee.salary;
}
```

Even DMN defines its own "for-loop" to express logic like "For employee in department <do something>".

READER. So, we cannot avoid programming in these cases, can we?

AUTHOR. Yes, we can. Today you will learn how OpenRules allows you to iterate through a collection of objects without explicitly defined a loop. Let's specify our business problem in more precise terms and try to build the proper decision model. So, let's say we have a department with many employees. The following Datatype table defines "Employee":

Datatype Employee	
String	name
int	age
String	gender
String	maritalStatus
int	salary
String	wealthCategory

Fig. 5-1. Datatype "Employee"

As we plan to accumulate different characteristics for all employees within a department, I will add the Datatype "Department":

Dialog-Session 5

Datatype Department	
String	department
Employee[]	employees
int	minSalary
int	maxSalary
int	totalSalary
int	numberOfHighPaidEmployees

Fig. 5-2. Datatype "Department"

READER. I see you are using the array type Employee[] in a manner similar to how we previously used String[].

AUTHOR. Right. I also want to apply business rules to determine values for minSalary, maxSalary, totalSalary, and the number of high-paid employees within a department.

READER. I understand that it is easy to define a rule for one employee to be considered as "high-paid" by checking if his/her salary is larger than a certain amount. But how will we do it for every employee?

AUTHOR. Just be patient – we are getting there.

Data Tables with References to Arrays

First, let's define our test data. The list of all employees in two departments of our fictitious organization is shown in Fig. 5-3. It is an array called "allEmployees" with elements of the type "Employee".

READER. But who belongs to which department?

Data Employee allEmployees

name	maritalStatus	gender	age	salary	wealthCategory
Name	Marital Status	Gender	Age	Salary	Wealth Category
Robinson	Married	Female	25	20000	?
Warner	Married	Male	45	150000	?
Stevens	Single	Male	24	35000	?
White	Married	Female	32	75000	?
Smith	Single	Male	46	110000	?
Green	Married	Female	28	40000	?
Brown	Married	Male	32	65000	?
Klaus	Married	Male	54	85000	?
Houston	Single	Female	47	35000	?
Long	Married	Male	29	40000	?
Short	Single	Male	22	20000	?
Doe	Single	Female	21	21000	?

Fig. 5-3. Data table "allEmployees"

AUTHOR. Let's define two departments in the following Data table:

Data Department departments

department	employees	minSalary	maxSalary	totalSalary	numberOfHighPaidEmployees
	>allEmployees				
Department	Employees	Min Salary	Max Salary	Total Salary	Number Of High-Paid Employees
Department 1	Robinson / Warner / Stevens / White / Smith / Green	0	0	0	0
Department 2	Brown / Klaus / Houston / Long / Short / Doe	0	0	0	0

Fig. 5-4. Data table "departments"

For each department, the second column "Employees" lists only those employees from the array "allEmployees" which belong to this department – one employee per sub-row. Please note that I added a reference **">allEmployees"** in the column "Employees" using an additional 3rd row.

READER. I guess the name of each employee must be unique. I also can see that you merged all sub-rows for other columns within each department's row.

AUTHOR, Yes, it is very important and at the same time quite intuitive. For example, by merging sub-rows for the row "Department 1" and the column "Min Salary", we explicitly show that this is the minimum salary for the all employees from Robinson to Green in the Department 1.

Now you should not have a problem putting together the glossary.

READER. Yes, let me try. Here is the glossary:

Glossary glossary		
Variable Name	**Business Concept**	**Attribute**
Name	Employee	name
Marital Status		age
Gender		gender
Age		maritalStatus
Salary		salary
Wealth Category		wealthCategory
Department	Department	department
Employees		employees
Min Salary		minSalary
Max Salary		maxSalary
Total Salary		totalSalary
Number Of High-Paid Employees		numberOfHighPaidEmployees

Fig. 5-5. Glossary

AUTHOR. Good. Now let's try to define high-paid employees. The decision table for one employee is shown in Fig. 5-6:

Evaluating One Element of Collection

DecisionTableMultiHit EvaluateOneEmployee				
Condition		Conclusion		Conclusion
Salary		Wealth Category		Number Of High-Paid Employees
>=	85000	Is	HighPaid	+=	1
<	85000	Is	Regular		

Fig. 5-6. Decision table "EvaluateOneEmployee"

READER. I believe I understand how the variable "Wealth Category" should be defined. It will be set to "HighPaid" for those who make 85K or more and to "Regular" for those who make less. But why did you use the "increment" operator "+=" to define the Number Of High-Paid Employees? Is it similar to what we did in scorecards?

AUTHOR. Yes and No. This operator still tells OpenRules to increment the variable "Number Of High-Paid Employees" by 1. However, each increment will take place, not for different satisfied rules, but rather for each employee for whom this decision table will be executed.

READER. So, this decision table can also be single-hit, correct?

AUTHOR. Yes, with the same results. Now, we want to execute this decision table for every employee within a selected department. How can we do it? OpenRules provides a special action called "**ActionIterate**" that can be used inside a regular decision table to iterate through an array or list of objects. Here is how we can use this action for our example:

Iterating Through All Elements of Collection

DecisionTable EvaluateAllEmployees					
Action	Action	Action	Action	ActionIterate	
Max Salary	Min Salary	Total Salary	Number Of High-Paid Employees	Array of Objects	Rules
0	1000000	0	0	Employees	EvaluateOne Employee

Fig. 5-7. Decision table "EvaluateAllEmployee"

The first 4 (regular) actions will simply initialize the variables in which we want to accumulate values for Max Salary, Min Salary, Total Salary, and Number Of High-Paid Employees. Then the last action of the type "ActionIterate" will execute our decision table "EvaluateOneEmployee" in Fig. 5-6 for every element of the array "Employees". The action "ActionIterate" uses 2 sub-columns:

1) **Array Of Objects** with the name of the array (e.g. Employees)
2) **Rules** with the name of the decision table that will be executed for each element of the array (e.g. EvaluateOneEmployee).

READER. I believe I understand how the decision tables "EvaluateAllEmployees" and "EvaluateOneEmployee" work together. For example, if we consider the variable "Number Of High-Paid Employees", then for every employee from the array "Employees" it will be incremented by 1 but only for employees with Salary >= 85000.

AUTHOR. That's a correct explanation.

READER. But our decision table "EvaluateOneEmployee" does not tell anything about other aggregated attributes: Min Salary, Max Salary, Total Salary, and Number Of Employees.

AUTHOR. You are right. Let's expand the decision table "EvaluateOneEmployee" to cover these variables as well. Here is the expanded table:

DecisionTableMultiHit EvaluateOneEmployee										
Condition		Conclusion		Conclusion		Conclusion		Conclusion	Conclusion	
Salary		Total Salary		Max Salary		Min Salary		Wealth Category	Number Of High-Paid Employees	
		+=	Salary	Max	Salary	Min	Salary			
>=	85000							Is	HighPaid	+=	1
<	85000							Is	Regular		

Fig. 5-8. Expanded Decision table "EvaluateOneEmployee"

READER. You've added 3 more conclusions. The first one will increment the variable "Total Salary" with the Salary of the currently considered employee. But you don't remember you telling me about "Max" and "Min" used in the 2nd and 3rd conclusions. Are they special operators?

AUTHOR. Exactly! And they are used to define the Maximal/Minimal value of an array's attributes.

READER. Got it. And now our table must be multi-hit, otherwise, the second and third rules will never be executed.

AUTHOR. That's absolutely correct.

READER. I am wondering why MIN Salary is initialized to 1000000...

AUTHOR. I've just used this number because it is larger than the salary of at least one any employee. The operator "Min" will use this number as a starting point for comparison, and the salary of the very first considered employee will override this number.

READER. Based on what they write about CEO's salaries of large conglomerates, probably it's safer to make it 100,000,000.

AUTHOR. Probably. Now, let's complete our decision model and try to run it. What are we still missing?

READER. We can use the usual file DecisionModel.xls. I've adjusted the file "build.bat" using these 3 parameters:

```
set GOAL="Total Salary"
set INPUT_FILE_NAME=rules/DecisionModel.xls
set OUTPUT_FILE_NAME=rules/Goals.xls
```

Fig. 5-9. Batch file "build.bat"

OOPS! When I double-clicked on "build.bat" it produced many warnings. Here is the first one:

```
Variable 'Min Salary' might be calculated by more than one decision
tables: EvaluateAllEmployees and EvaluateOneEmployee

*** WARNING: AUTOMATICALLY GENERATED EXECUTION PATH MAY
CONTAIN ERRORS - PLEASE CHECK!!!
```

Fig. 5-10. Building warnings

AUTHOR. This is the correct warning because usually each decision variable should be defined by only one decision table. However, many of our variables are defined in both decision tables "EvaluateAllEmployees" and "EvaluateOneEmployee". Please look at the file "Goals.xls" that is still being generated. As you can see, It invokes only table "EvaluateAllEmployees" and not "EvaluateOneEmployee". So, in this case, we may ignore all similar warnings. However, when you use iterations it's always a good idea to check the generated path.

READER. What if I still want to use a decision variable in conclusions of two or more regular decision tables (without iterations)?

AUTHOR. Usually, people try to avoid such situations and DMN even requires that a variable can be determined by only one decision table. OpenRules allows you to use the same decision variable in conclusions of different decision tables, however, in this case instead of relying on "build.bat", you should create your execution path in the file "Goals.xls" manually.

READER. Got it. Now we need to add the table "testCases". We will use two test cases one for each department. As it's hard to calculate manually the expected results, I'd not use them in the table (at least initially):

DecisionTableTest testCases	
#	ActionUseObject
Test ID	Department
Test 1	:= departments[0]
Test 2	:= departments[1]

Fig. 5-11. Test Cases

AUTHOR. That's OK, you may check the actually produced results and if they are OK, you will add them to this table as expected results later.

Executing Decision Tables with Iterations

READER. I will. To execute this decision model, I need to modify its file "run.bat" by setting the parameter DECISION_NAME to DecisionTotalSalary. Now I will double-click on this file to run our model. The execution results for Test 1 are in Fig. 5-12.

AUTHOR. Please explain this execution protocol.

READER. I will try. The first 4 Assign-statements initialize our decision variables – it's done by the decision table "EvaluateAllEmpoyees". Then the iteration over Employees starts applying the rules "EvaluateOneEmployee" to every one of our 6 employees in Department 1. We can see not all but only some of the actually executed rule conclusions, e.g.

```
Number of High-Paid Employees += 1
Wealth Category id HighPaid
```

As we didn't have any "ActionExpect" columns in our table "testCases", Test 1 was successful. And probably it is!

AUTHOR. Now you can add the expected results.

READER. How would I know the expected results?

AUTHOR. Usually, you need to calculate them manually even before you implement the rules. However, in this case, if you already trust our decision model, use already calculated results as expected.

READER. I did it, and both tests work fine.

```
RUN TEST: Test 1
  Assign: Max Salary = 0
  Assign: Min Salary = 1000000
  Assign: Total Salary = 0
  Assign: Number Of High-Paid Employees = 0
Iterate over Employees using rules EvaluateOneEmployee
  Conclusion: Total Salary += 20000
  Conclusion: Max Salary Max 20000
  Conclusion: Min Salary Min 20000
  Conclusion: Wealth Category Is Regular
  Conclusion: Total Salary += 170000
  Conclusion: Max Salary Max 150000
  Conclusion: Min Salary Min 20000
  Conclusion: Number Of High-Paid Employees += 1
  Conclusion: Wealth Category Is HighPaid
  Conclusion: Total Salary += 205000
  Conclusion: Max Salary Max 150000
  Conclusion: Min Salary Min 20000
  Conclusion: Wealth Category Is Regular
  Conclusion: Total Salary += 280000
  Conclusion: Max Salary Max 150000
  Conclusion: Min Salary Min 20000
  Conclusion: Wealth Category Is Regular
  Conclusion: Total Salary += 390000
  Conclusion: Max Salary Max 150000
  Conclusion: Min Salary Min 20000
  Conclusion: Number Of High-Paid Employees += 2
  Conclusion: Wealth Category Is HighPaid
  Conclusion: Total Salary += 430000
  Conclusion: Max Salary Max 150000
  Conclusion: Min Salary Min 20000
  Conclusion: Wealth Category Is Regular
Validating results for the test <Test 1>
Test 1 was successful
```

Fig. 5-12. Execution Results for Test 1

AUTHOR. Very good! Now we will try to solve another DMCommunity Challenge called "Order Promotions" that deals with more complex iterations.

Decision Model "Order Promotions"

AUTHOR. This challenge deals with a real-world business problem that many merchants face every day: define various promotions for their sales orders. An order usually consists of order items with known price and quantities. A promotion defines minimal quantities of certain items in the eligible orders. The challenge provided this example of promotion:

Reduce the total cost of the order by $3.50 if it contains at least 5 items 1108 and at least 4 items 2639.

Our decision model should automatically decide if a particular order is eligible to promotions similar to this one. What is your first impression?

READER. The promotion itself sounds simple enough and we can define the top-level goal as "**Order Is Eligible for Promotion**" with possible answers "Yes" or "No". However, there are too many concepts involved... and it's unclear to me how to proceed.

AUTHOR. To determine if an order is eligible for a promotion we need to check if the order's items cover the promotion's requirements, but his process may involve embedded iterations. I can give you some practical advice. **When a problem is difficult to understand, it always makes sense to start with test data** instead of jumping to the business logic. Putting together examples of orders and promotions will help us to better understand the problem itself.

We will use Excel Data tables in the OpenRules format. Please create a new project "OrderPromotion" and we will put our traditional Data and Datatype tables in the file "rules/Test.xls".

Defining Test Examples

AUTHOR. Let's start with some sales items. Probably each item has a unique id like "1108" or "2639" and a price. Let's create a Data table with some items.

READER. OK. I placed some items in the following list:

Data Item items	
id	price
Item Id	Item Price
1108	$4.25
1112	$3.50
1610	$5.00
1723	$1.80
2456	$2.50
2639	$3.75

Fig. 5-13. Example of sales items

AUTHOR. Good. Now you may create the corresponding Datatype table.

READER. It's easy:

Datatype Item	
String	id
double	price

Fig. 5-14. Datatype "Item"

AUTHOR. Good. Now let's create several orders. Each order has a unique id, say "AAA" and "BBB" and an array of order items included in the order. I'd recommend first to create a list of order item such as in Fig. 5-15:

Data OrderItem orderItems		
id	itemId	qty
Order Id-Item Id	Item Id	Qty
AAA-1108	1108	5
AAA-1112	1112	3
AAA-2639	2639	6
AAA-2456	2456	7
BBB-2639	2639	4
BBB-1108	1108	7

Fig. 5-15. An array of Order Items

READER. I understand that each order item contains an Item Id from our list in Fig. 5-13 and the quantity ("Qty") of these items inside an order. But why did you create the column for the pair Order Id-Item ID?

AUTHOR. Because we need a unique ID for each Order Item that we will be used when we refer to it inside the order. You will understand it better when I show you a list of Orders:

Data Order orders	
orderId	orderItems
	>orderItems
Order Id	Order Items
AAA	AAA-1108
	AAA-1112
	AAA-2639
	AAA-2456
BBB	BBB-2639
	BBB-1108

Fig. 5-16. An array of Orders with references to Order Items

READER. Now I understand. In this table, you are using the 3rd row with a reference ">orderItems" to all order items defined in the table 5-15.

AUTHOR. It should be easy for you to add Datatype tables for type "OrderItem" and "Order".

READER. Here they are:

Datatype OrderItem	
String	id
String	itemId
String	qty

Fig. 5-17. Datatype "OrderItem"

Datatype Order	
String	orderId
OrderItem[]	orderItems

Fig. 5-18. Datatype "Order"

AUTHOR. Now let's consider promotions. What each promotion item should contain at the very minimum?

READER. Based on the provided example, each promotion item contains an Item Id like "1108" or "2639" and the minimally required quantity of this item inside an order, e.g. 5 or 4.

AUTOR. Right. Now you can add lists of Promotion Items and Promotions in the same way as we did for Order Items and Orders.

READER. OK, here is my Data table "promotionItems":

Data PromotionItem promotionItems		
id	itemId	minQty
Promotion-Item	**Item Id**	**Minimal Qty**
Promo1-1108	1108	5
Promo1-2639	2639	4
Promo2-1112	1112	3
Promo2-1723	1723	4
Promo2-1610	1610	2

Fig. 5-19. Example of two promotion items

AUTHOR. Very good. We will use the first two promotion items to define the provided promotion called "Promo1". And 3 remaining promotion items will define the second promotion "Promo2".

READER. I also gave each promotion item a unique ID in the first column that consists of Promotion ID – Item Id. We will use these IDs to refer to the promotion items in the following list of promotions:

Data Promotion promotions	
id	promotionItems
	>promotionItems
Promotion Id	Promotion Items
Promo1	Promo1-1108
	Promo1-2639
Promo2	Promo2-1112
	Promo2-1723
	Promo2-1610

Fig. 5-20. An array of Promotions with references to Promotion Items

AUTHOR. Good job! It seems by now you understand well how one Data table can refer to an array defined in another table. Please specify the Datatype table for "PromotionItem" and "Promotion".

READER. Here they are:

Datatype PromotionItem	
String	id
String	itemId
int	minQty

Fig. 5-21. Datatype "PromotionItem"

Datatype Promotion	
String	id
PromotionItem[]	promotionItems

Fig. 5-22. Datatype "Promotion"

AUTHOR. Very good. Looking at these 2 orders (Figures 5-15 and 5-16) and 2 promotions (Figures 5-19 and 5-20) will you be able to explain which orders are eligible to which promotions?

READER. Let me try. Let's start with Order AAA. To be eligible for Promotion "Promo1", it needs to include at least 5 items 1108 and at least 4 items 2639. And Fig. 5-15 shows that it does include 5 items 1108 and 6 items 2639 (that is more than minimally required 4 items). So, the order AAA is eligible to Promo1. But Promotion "Promo2" requires at least 4 items 1723 but Order 1 does not include any. So, the order AAA is not eligible to Promo2.

AUTHOR. A very clear and straightforward logic! I am sure you may similarly conclude that order BBB is eligible to "Promo1" but not to "Promo2". I believe that now when we have clearly specified examples of orders, promotions, and relationships between them, we should be able to get back to the representation of business logic using goals and decision tables.

READER. Shouldn't I also add the test cases?

AUTHOR. Yes. Please do and we will be ready to continue with business logic.

READER. Each test case in the following table contain a combination of an order and a promotion:

DecisionTableTest testCases			
#	ActionUseObject	ActionUseObject	ActionExpect
Test ID	Order	Promotion	Order is Eligible for Promotion
Test-1	:= orders[0]	:= promotions[0]	YES
Test-2	:= orders[0]	:= promotions[1]	NO
Test-3	:= orders[1]	:= promotions[0]	YES
Test-4	:= orders[1]	:= promotions[1]	NO

Fig. 5-23. Test Cases

AUTHOR. So, for each test case, our decision model will receive one order and one promotion. To decide if an order is eligible for a promotion we need to check if every promotion item is present in the order in a sufficient quantity.

READER. To be more specific, we should check if the quantity of each promotion item inside the order is greater than its minimally required quantity.

AUTHOR. Let's present this logic in a decision table called "ComparePromotionItemAndOrderQuantities" assuming that it deals with a Promotion Item and an Order Item. This table should define a new decision variable "Promotion Item Quantity Minimum Satisfied" that will belong to the business concept "PromotionItem".

READER. Do you mean a decision table like this one?

DecisionTable ComparePromotionItemAndOrderQuantities				
Condition		Condition		Action
Promotion Item Id		Promotion Item Minimal Qty		Promotion Item Quantity Minimum Satisfied
=	Order Item Id	<=	Order Item Qty	YES

Fig. 5-24. Decision Table to compare promotion and Order Items

AUTHOR. Looks good. We need to execute this table for each promotion item and for each order item. Assuming that we already know the current Promotion Item, how can we iterate through all order items and call this table? In other words, how would you organize such iteration?

READER. I can use a decision table with **ActionIterate** that will iterate through the array Order Items similarly to what we did to evaluate all employees <u>above</u>. For example, we may do it using the following decision table:

DecisionTable EvaluatePromotionItemAgainstOrderItem	
ActionIterate	
Array of Objects	Rules
Order Items	ComparePromotionItemAndOrderQuantities

Fig. 5-25. Decision Table for iteration through Order Items

AUTHOR. This "iteration loop" looks good, and it will execute decision table 5-24 for every order item. However, what if no rules will be executed for any order item? More specifically: what value will be assigned to the variable "Promotion Item Quantity Minimum Satisfied"?

READER. It should be "NO" but where can we define this default value?

AUTHOR. Do you remember how we initialized some decision variable before using them inside an iteration loop? Look again at Fig. <u>5-7</u>.

READER. Aha! I can simply add this initialization as the first action in my decision table 5-25. Here is the modified table:

DecisionTable EvaluatePromotionItemAgainstOrderItem		
Action	ActionIterate	
Promotion Item Quantity Minimum Satisfied	Array of Objects	Rules
NO	Order Items	ComparePromotionItemAndOrderQuantities

Fig. 5-26. Decision Table for iteration through Promotion Items with Initialization

AUTHOR. Very good. But we made an assumption that when we run this "iteration loop" (decision table 5-26) we should already know the current Promotion Item. It means that we need to put this loop inside another loop that iterates through all promotion items.

READER. I can do it similarly just for the array "Promotion Items" that should be a part of every Promotion.

AUTHOR. Of course, and you do not need any initialization in this case. You may call your new "loop" "DefinePromotionItemSatisfaction":

DecisionTable DefinePromotionItemSatisfaction	
ActionIterate	
Array of Objects	Rules
Promotion Items	EvaluatePromotionItemAgainstOrderItem

Fig. 5-27. Decision Table for iteration through Promotion Items

AUTHOR. Good. By executing this decision table, we will define the variable "Promotion Item Quantity Minimum Satisfied" as "YES" or "NO" for every promotion item relatively to our order. Then we can iterate again through all promotion items and if for at least one item the variable "Promotion Item Quantity Minimum Satisfied" has the value "NO" we should set our top-level goal "Order is Eligible To Promotion" to "NO".

READER. I got it. We can again loop through promotion items, and execute the following decision table for each promotion item:

DecisionTable ApplyPromotionItemQuantityMinimumSatisfied	
If	Then
Promotion Item Quantity Minimum Satisfied	Order is Eligible for Promotion
NO	NO

Fig. 5-28. Decision Table for iteration through Promotion Items

AUTHOR. Exactly! And what should be a default value for our goal?

READER. Of course, it should be "YES". Here is my new loop with such initialization:

DecisionTable ApplyPromotionItemSatisfaction		
Action	ActionIterate	
Order is Eligible for Promotion	Array of Objects	Rules
YES	Promotion Items	ApplyPromotionItemQuantityMinimumSatisfied

Fig. 5-29. Another Iteration Loop through Promotion Items

AUTHOR. Great! This completes our business logic.

READER. Wow! After all, it does not look so difficult as I was afraid of. Using tables with "ActionIterate" to represent "iteration loops" makes everything much more intuitive.

AUTHOR. I am glad you like it. Now, let's finally put all introduced decision variables to our glossary. Which business concepts will we use?

READER. Our top-level goal "Order is Eligible for Promotion" probably belongs to the business concept "Order". The Order should also contain an array "Order Items". We will need the business concept "OrderItem" with item's Id and Quantity. Similarly, we will need business concepts "Promotion" and "PromotionItem". My version of the Glossary is presented in Fig. 5-30.

AUTHOR. Looks good to me. Our test data is already in place. Wait, as we've added the variable "Promotion Item Quantity Minimum Satisfied", we need to add the corresponding attribute "qtyMinimumSatisfied" to the Datatype "PromotionItem".

Glossary glossary		
Variable Name	**Business Concept**	**Attribute**
Order Items	Order	orderItems
Order is Eligible for Promotion		orderEligibleForPromotion
Order Item Id	OrderItem	itemId
Order Item Qty		qty
Promotion Items	Promotion	promotionItems
Promotion Amount		amount
Promotion Item Id	PromotionItem	itemId
Promotion Item Minimal Qty		minQty
Promotion Item Quantity Minimum Satisfied		qtyMinimumSatisfied

Fig. 5-30. Glossary

READER. Done. Now I will adjust the batch-file "build.bat" using GOAL="Order is Eligible for Promotion". Let me double-click on this file to build our decision model. I see two warnings, but you said that in case of iterations we may ignore them.

AUTHOR. Just in case, check out the generated file "Goals.xls".

READER. It shows this execution path:

Decision DecisionOrderisEligibleforPromotion
ActionExecute
Decision Tables
DefinePromotionItemSatisfaction
ApplyPromotionItemSatisfaction

Fig. 5-31. Generated Execution Path

So, first OpenRules will execute "DefinePromotionSatisfaction" and then "ApplyPromotionSatisfaction". This is exactly what we want.

AUTHOR. Adjust "run.bat" and you may run our test cases through these two iteration loops.

READER. The execution results (Fig.5-32 shows Test-3 and Test-4) look good.

```
RUN TEST: Test-3 2019-02-13 13:38:22.882
Execute DefinePromotionItemSatisfaction
Iterate over Promotion Items using rules EvaluatePromotionItemAgainstO
  Assign: Promotion Item Quantity Minimum Satisfied = NO
Iterate over Order Items using rules ComparePromotionItemAndOrderQuant
  Assign: Promotion Item Quantity Minimum Satisfied = YES
  Assign: Promotion Item Quantity Minimum Satisfied = NO
Iterate over Order Items using rules ComparePromotionItemAndOrderQuant
  Assign: Promotion Item Quantity Minimum Satisfied = YES
Execute ApplyPromotionItemSatisfaction
  Assign: Order is Eligible for Promotion = YES
Iterate over Promotion Items using rules ApplyPromotionItemQuantityMin
Validating results for the test <Test-3>
Test-3 was successful
Executed test Test-3 in 17 ms

RUN TEST: Test-4 2019-02-13 13:38:22.901
Execute DefinePromotionItemSatisfaction
Iterate over Promotion Items using rules EvaluatePromotionItemAgainstO
  Assign: Promotion Item Quantity Minimum Satisfied = NO
Iterate over Order Items using rules ComparePromotionItemAndOrderQuant
  Assign: Promotion Item Quantity Minimum Satisfied = NO
Iterate over Order Items using rules ComparePromotionItemAndOrderQuant
  Assign: Promotion Item Quantity Minimum Satisfied = NO
Iterate over Order Items using rules ComparePromotionItemAndOrderQuant
Execute ApplyPromotionItemSatisfaction
  Assign: Order is Eligible for Promotion = YES
Iterate over Promotion Items using rules ApplyPromotionItemQuantityMin
  Assign: Order is Eligible for Promotion = NO
  Assign: Order is Eligible for Promotion = NO
  Assign: Order is Eligible for Promotion = NO
Validating results for the test <Test-4>
Test-4 was successful
```

Fig. 5-32. Generated Execution Path

AUTHOR. Very good. Business logic defined on collections of objects is usually among complex decision modeling problems, but it seems you did well today.

READER. Thank you. I'd not say it was not simple, but now I feel quite comfortable with those notorious "iteration loops".

Suggested Exercises

1. Enhance the model "AggregatedValues" by adding and calculating "Number of Low-Paid Employees".

2. Analyze and execute the decision model "PartyAdmissionPolicy"

Dialog-Session 6: Building and Using Domain-Specific Libraries of Decision Models

Discussed Topics:

Related OpenRules Project:

LoanOrigination

AUTHOR. Nice to see you again. I assume that by now you feel comfortable using the Goal-Oriented approach to decision modeling. During our previous sessions, we build quite a few decision models and did it every time from scratch covering all details including business logic and test cases. However, in real-world situations, people prefer not to build everything from scratch but to reuse already created decision models.

Usually, OpenRules customers build not one but multiple operational business decision models within their specific business domains like property and casualty insurance, loan origination, medical guidelines, etc. After building one or two decision models, they usually already have a quite rich glossary that covers many concepts in their business domain. So, they build a library of relatively small decision models which can be used to assemble more complex decision models. Sometimes they add domain-specific decision tables and supporting Java classes. Today we will create a small library of decision models for the loan origination problems and will learn how to use this library to assemble larger decision models.

READER. I believe we will do something similar in our business domain as it does not make sense reinventing the wheel for every decision model and every business goal. I've already started to play with an idea of building a centralized business glossary and datatypes that can be reused across our multiple lines of business.

AUTHOR. Very good. We will limit our today's session to loan origination problems described in Chapter 11 of the DMN specification [1] that specifies business logic behind the loan origination process presented in Fig. 6-1. The process handles an application for a loan, obtaining data from a credit bureau only if required for the case, and automatically deciding whether the application should be accepted, declined, or referred for human review.

There are several sources of input data for decision-making: (Requested product, Applicant data, and Bureau data), and two major decisions (Bureau Strategy and Routing). Between the two are intermediate decisions: evaluation of risk, affordability, and eligibility.

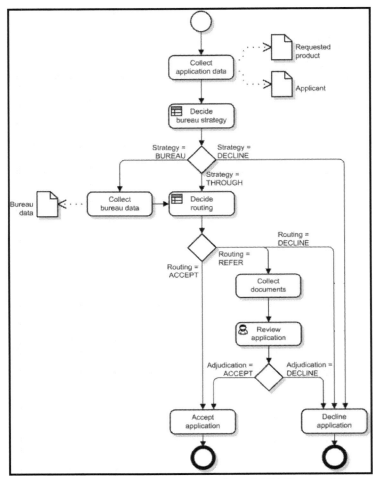

Fig. 6-1. Loan Origination Process from DMN Chapter 11

There are different implementations of decision models supporting this process created in response to the June-2017 Challenge.

Our objective is not to directly implement these decision models from scratch, but rather to demonstrate how to create and use a library of decision models that cover the problems from this domain. So, here is a more specific plan for today:

1) We will build a library of decision models that can determine the following goals:
   a. Application Risk Score
   b. Pre-Bureau Risk Strategy
   c. Post-Bureau Risk Strategy
   d. Affordability.
2) We will use these decision models to assemble decision models for the goals:
   a. Bureau Strategy
   b. Routing.
3) We will use these decision models to create a decision model for "Loan Origination Result".

I will quickly show you the models for Step 1, and then we will together concentrate on the different assembly methods during Steps 2 and 3.

READER. Sounds like a good plan. I will jump in if I have any questions.

Building a Library of Decision Models

AUTHOR. First, we will create a central repository which will have separate sub-folders for different goals. Inside the project folder "LoanOrigination" we create a folder "repository" with two sub-folders "Decisions" and "Tests". Inside these sub-folders, we will create sub-folders for every decision model, e.g. "BureauStrategy", "Routing", etc.

- LoanOrigination
  - Repository
    - Decisions
      - BureauStrategy
      - Routing
    - Tests
      - BureauStrategy
      - Routing

Let's start with a very simple decision model that does not depend on any other model.

Decision Model "Application Risk Score"

I've created the folder "Decisions/ApplicationRiskScore/" with the file "Rules.xls". This file contains only one decision table presented in Fig. 6-2. Any comments?

DecisionTableMultiHit ApplicationRiskScore				
If	If	If	Conclusion	
Age	Marital Status	Employment Status	Application Risk Score	
			=	0
[18..21]			+=	32
[22..25]			+=	35
[26..35]			+=	40
[36..49]			+=	43
>=50			+=	48
	S		+=	25
	M		+=	45
		UNEMPLOYED	+=	15
		STUDENT	+=	18
		EMPLOYED	+=	45
		SELF-EMPLOYED	+=	36

Fig. 6-2. Decision Table "ApplicationRiskScore"

READER. This is a typical scorecard implemented as a multi-hit decision table. The first rule initializes the variable "Application Risk Score" and other rules may increment its value based on different values of Applicant's Age, Marital Status, and Employment Status.

AUTHOR. Good. Contrary to the file organization used in our previous sessions, now all decision models included in our future library should share the same Glossary. So, I will place it into the file "Decisions/Glossary/Glossary.xls". Here is the initial Glossary created based on this decision table only:

Glossary glossary		
Variable	**Business Concept**	**Attribute**
Age		age
Marital Status	Applicant	maritalStatus
Employment Status		employmentStatus
Application Risk Score	Application	applicationRiskScore

Fig. 6-3. Initial Glossary

AUTHOR. As usual, we need the file "DecisionModel.xls" inside the folder "Decisions/ApplicationRiskScore/" with the Environment table:

Environment	
include	Rules.xls
	../Glossary/Glossary.xls

Fig. 6-4. The Environment table refers to the common Glossary

Please note that this Environment table doesn't contain an include-statement to the standard OpenRules templates that in this case may refer to

../../../../openrules.config/DecisionTemplates.xls

As "../Glossary/Glossary.xls" will be included in all Environment tables inside our library, I've already added an Environment table directly to the file "Glossary.xls". It contains only one "include" that refers to DecisionTemplates.xls.

The folder "Decisions/ApplicationRiskScore/" will also contain the file "build.bat" that allows us to build this decision model and to generate "Goals.xls":

```
set GOAL="Application Risk Score"
set INPUT_FILE_NAME=repository/Decisions/ApplicationRiskScore/DecisionModel.xls
set OUTPUT_FILE_NAME=repository/Decisions/ApplicationRiskScore/Goals.xls
```

Fig. 6-5. The settings inside the batch-file "build.bat"

To test this decision model, we will use the file "Test.xls" placed in the folder "repository/**Tests**/ApplicationRiskScore/". To refer to our decision model his file includes its own Environment table:

Environment	
include	../../Decisions/ApplicationRiskScore/Goals.xls

Fig. 6-6. The Environment table in "Test.xls"

All related Datatype, Data, and DecisionTableTest tables for this decision model are shown in Fig. 6-7.

Data Applicant applicants

fullName	age	maritalStatus	employmentStatus
Borrower Full Name	Age	Marital Status	Employment Status
Peter N. Johnson	51	M	EMPLOYED
Mary K. Brown	24	S	STUDENT
Robert Cooper Jr.	59	Other	UNEMPLOYED

Datatype Applicant

String	fullName
int	age
String	maritalStatus
String	employmentStatus

Data Application applications

id	applicationRiskScore
ID	Application Risk Score
1	0
2	0
3	0

Datatype Application

String	id
int	applicationRiskScore

DecisionTableTest testCases

#	ActionUseObject	ActionUseObject	ActionExpect
Test ID	Applicant	Application	Application Risk Score
Test 1	:= applicants[0]	:= applications[0]	138
Test 2	:= applicants[1]	:= applications[1]	78
Test 3	:= applicants[2]	:= applications[2]	63

Fig. 6-7. Test tables for "ApplicationRiskScore"

Now we only need to adjust the batch-file "run.bat" as in Fig. 6-8 and run our little model. The execution results are presented in Fig. 6-9.

```
set DECISION_NAME=DecisionApplicationRiskScore
set FILE_NAME=repository/Tests/ApplicationRiskScore/Test.xls
```

Fig. 6-8. The settings inside the batch-file "run.bat"

```
RUN TEST: Test 1
  Conclusion: Application Risk Score =0
  Conclusion: Application Risk Score +=48
  Conclusion: Application Risk Score +=93
  Conclusion: Application Risk Score +=138
Validating results for the test <Test 1>
Test 1 was successful
```

Fig. 6-9. The execution results for Test 1

READER. Everything you had shown is very familiar now.

AUTHOR. Good. For other 3 decision models I will show only decision tables and the updated glossary.

Decision Model "Pre-Bureau Risk Category"

Usually, a loan origination process should include pre-bureau and post-bureau sub-processes that define so-called "Risk Category". The first one does this before a credit score of the applicant is known and the second one – after. Let's start with pre-bureau processing.

In this case "Risk Category" can be defined by the decision table in Fig. 6-10 which I placed in the file "Rules.xls" inside the folder "repository/Decisions/PreBureauRiskCategory/". Actually, this is a straight-forward representation of the decision table "Pre-bureau Risk Category" from the DMN's Specification in the OpenRules format.

DecisionTable PreBureauRiskCategory		
Condition	If	Then
Existing Customer	Application Risk Score	Risk Category
Is	<100	HIGH
Is	[100..120)	MEDIUM
Is	[120..130]	LOW
Is	>130	VERY LOW
Is	<80	DECLINE
Is	[80..90)	HIGH
Is	[90..110]	MEDIUM
Is	>110	LOW

Fig. 6-10. Defining Risk Category for Pre-Bureau Processing

READER. Everything is clear and simple here. We just need to add new variables to our common glossary.

AUTHOR. Here it is:

Glossary glossary		
Variable	Business Concept	Attribute
Age		age
Marital Status	Applicant	maritalStatus
Employment Status		employmentStatus
Existing Customer		existingCustomer
Application Risk Score	Application	applicationRiskScore
Risk Category		riskCategory

Fig. 6-11. Adjusted Glossary

But this is not all. The above decision table uses "Application Risk Score". So, we need to include our previous decision model inside this one. It can be done simply by modifying the file "Decisions/PreBureauRiskCategory/DecisionModel.xls". Its Environment table should include a reference to the decision model "ApplicationRiskScore" as in Fig. 6-12:

Environment	
include	Rules.xls
	../ApplicationRiskScore/DecisionModel.xls

Fig. 6-12. The Environment table for "PreBureauRiskCategory"

READER. Wow! How will it work? And why you haven't included Glossary.xls?

AUTHOR. As we discussed earlier, the file "DecisionModel.xls" is usually an entry point to any decision model that refers to all other included components. We've included the file "../ApplicationRiskScore/DecisionModel.xls" that already refers to the common glossary file and the standard OpenRules templates, so there are no needs to repeat them here.

READER. That's great!

AUTHOR. You may trust me that when I created the tests and run them, I received the expected results.

Decision Model "Post-Bureau Risk Category"

So, now our library already includes two decision models. Let's add another one for post-bureau processing.

In this case "Risk Category" can be defined by the decision table in Fig. 6-13 which I placed in the file "Rules.xls" inside the folder "repository/Decisions/PostBureauRiskCategory/".

DecisionTable PostBureauRiskCategory				
Condition		If	If	Then
Existing Customer		Application Risk Score	Credit Score	Risk Category
Is	TRUE	< 120	<590	HIGH
Is			[590..610]	MEDIUM
Is			>610	LOW
Is		[120..130]	<600	HIGH
Is			[600..625]	MEDIUM
Is			>625	LOW
Is		> 130		VERY LOW
Is	FALSE	<=100	<580	HIGH
Is			[580..600]	MEDIUM
Is			>600	LOW
Is		>100	<590	HIGH
Is			[590..615]	MEDIUM
Is			>615	LOW

Fig. 6-13. Defining Risk Category for Post-Bureau Processing

This table uses "Credit Score" that belongs to the business concept "BureauData". Here is the adjusted Glossary:

Glossary glossary		
Variable	Business Concept	Attribute
Age	Applicant	age
Marital Status		maritalStatus
Employment Status		employmentStatus
Existing Customer		existingCustomer
Application Risk Score	Application	applicationRiskScore
Risk Category		riskCategory
Bureau Name	BureauData	bureauName
Credit Score		creditScore

Fig. 6-14. Common Glossary adjusted for post-bureau processing

Like the table in Fig. 6-10, this model also depends on the decision variable "Application Risk Score". It means it can be similarly connected to the decision model "ApplicationRiskScore". So, we can use exactly the same file "DecisionModel.xls" just placed in the folder "Decisions/PostBureauRiskCategory/".

READER. So far I have no problem following you.

AUTHOR. Very good. I just want to remind you that all decision variables should have unique names and now we use the same variable "Risk Category" inside two different decision models "PreBureauRiskCategory" and "PostBureauRiskCategory". It means we have to be careful to never include both these models at the same time as a part of a high-level decision model.

Decision Model "Affordability"

Now it's time to add one more decision model to our library. The goal of this decision model is called "Affordability" and is defined in the DMN specification using the following decision table:

DecisionTable Affordability	
If	**Then**
Required Monthly Installment	**Affordability**
< Disposable Income * Credit Contingency Factor	TRUE
	FALSE

Fig. 6-15. Decision table "Affordability"

This decision table uses 3 subgoals to calculate "Affordability":
- Disposable Income

- Required Monthly Installment
- Credit Contingency Factor.

We will define these subgoals one by one. Here is the decision table for the subgoal "Disposable Income":

DecisionTable DisposableIncome
Action
Disposable Income
Monthly Income - (Monthly Repayments + Monthly Expenses)

Fig. 6-16. Decision table "Disposable Income"

And here is the one for the subgoal "Required Monthly Installment":

DecisionTable RequiredMonthlyInstallment		
Condition		Action
Product Type		Required Monthly Installment
Is	SPECIAL LOAN	PMT + 25.00
		PMT + 20.00

Fig. 6-17. Decision table "Required Monthly Installment"

This decision table uses the decision variable (subgoal) "PMT" that can be calculated using this decision table:

DecisionTable PMT
Action
PMT
(Amount * Rate/12) / (1 - (1 +Rate/12) ** -Term)

Fig. 6-18. Calculating PMT

The only remaining undefined subgoal is "Credit Contingency Factor". Here is a decision table for its calculation:

DecisionTable CreditContingencyFactor		
Condition		Action
Risk Category		Credit Contingency Factor
Is One Of	HIGH,DECLINE	0.6
Is	MEDIUM	0.7
Is One Of	LOW, VERY LOW	0.8

Fig. 6-19. Decision table "Credit Contingency Factor"

I placed all these 5 decision tables in the file "Rules.xls" inside "repository/Decisions/Affordability/".

Now, we need to address the following issue. The last Affordability's subgoal "Credit Contingency Factor" depends on "Risk Category", for which we already have two decision models:
- PreBureauRiskCategory
- PostBureauRiskCategory.

When we calculate "Affordability" for pre-bureau processing we want to use Risk Category defined by the first decision model, and we want to use the second model for post-bureau processing. How could we do it?

READER. Previously we defined which decision model to be used by an include-statement in the table "Environment" in the file "DecisionModel.xls". However, we have only one file "DecisionModel.xls" …

AUTHOR. Nothing prevents us to create two different files:
- DecisionModelPreBureau.xls
- DecisionModelPostBureau.xls

The first one will use this Environment table:

Environment	
include	Rules.xls
	../PreBureauRiskCategory/DecisionModel.xls

Fig. 6-20. The Environment table in DecisionModelPreBureau.xls

And the second one will use this Environment table:

Environment	
include	Rules.xls
	../PostBureauRiskCategory/DecisionModel.xls

Fig. 6-21. The Environment table in DecisionModelPostBureau.xls

READER. Aha, so we can have two different build files - one, let's call it "buildPreBureau.bat", can build the PreBureau model, and the other, "buildPostBureau.bat" - can build PostBureau model. Here is the file "buildPreBureau.bat":

```
set GOAL="Affordability"
set INPUT_FILE_NAME=repository/Decisions/Affordability/DecisionModelPreBureau.xls
set OUTPUT_FILE_NAME=repository/Decisions/Affordability/GoalsPreBureau.xls
```

Fig. 6-22. Settings for the batch file "buildPreBureau.xls"

And the file "buildPostBureau.bat" looks similarly but uses DecisionModelPostBureau.xls as INPUT_FILE_NAME and GoalsPostBureau.xls as OUTPUT_FILE_NAME. These batch-files will generate two different decision models in the files "GoalsPreBureau.xls" and "GoalsPostBureau.xls".

AUTHOR. Very good! So, now our library will contain 5 decision models:

- Application Risk Score
- Pre-Bureau Risk Strategy
- Post-Bureau Risk Strategy
- Affordability for Pre-Bureau Processing
- Affordability for Post-Bureau Processing.

We just need to update our common Glossary as it's shown in Fig. 6-23.

Glossary glossary		
Variable	**Business Concept**	**Attribute**
Age		age
Marital Status		maritalStatus
Employment Status		employmentStatus
Monthly Income	Applicant	monthlyIncome
Monthly Repayments		monthlyRepayments
Monthly Expenses		monthlyExpenses
Existing Customer		existingCustomer
Application Risk Score		applicationRiskScore
Risk Category		riskCategory
PMT		pmt
Required Monthly Installment	Application	requiredMonthlyInstallment
Disposable Income		disposableIncome
Credit Contingency Factor		creditContingencyFactor
Affordability		affordability
Product Type		productType
Amount		amount
Rate	RequestedProduct	rate
Term		term
Bureau Name		bureauName
Credit Score	BureauData	creditScore

Fig. 6-23. Updated glossary for the library of 5 decision models

I will not show separate test-cases for all these models, but you may run them yourself after this session because you have access to all files inside "repository/Decisions/Affordability/" and "repository/Tests/Affordability". Now we can say that our library is ready to be used to assemble higher level decision models.

Assembling Decision Model "Bureau Strategy"

First, we will use our library to assemble the decision model "Bureau Strategy" in the folder "repository/Decisions/BureauStrategy/". This decision model implements pre-bureau processing for the high-level loan origination process.

Following the DMN Chapter 11, we may define the goal "Bureau Strategy" in the following decision table:

DecisionTable BureauStrategy					
Condition		Condition		Action	
Eligibility		Bureau Call Type		Bureau Strategy	
Is	INELIGIBLE			DECLINE	
Is	ELIGIBLE	Is One Of	FULL, MINI	BUREAU	
Is		Is	NONE	THROUGH	

Fig. 6-24. Decision table "Bureau Strategy"

As you can see, the goal "Bureau Strategy" depends on two subgoals "Eligibility" and "Bureau Call Type". The subgoal "Bureau Call Type" can be defined by the following decision table:

DecisionTable BureauCallType			
Condition		Action	
Risk Category		Bureau Call Type	
Is One Of	HIGH,MEDIUM	FULL	
Is	LOW	MINI	
Is One Of	VERY LOW, DECLINE	NONE	

Fig. 6-25. Decision table "BureauCallType"

The subgoal "Eligibility" can be defined by the following decision table:

DecisionTable Eligibility			
If	If	If	Then
Risk Category	**Affordability**	**Age**	**Eligibility**
DECLINE	-	-	INELIGIBLE
-	FALSE		INELIGIBLE
-	-	<18	INELIGIBLE
-	-	-	ELIGIBLE

Fig. 6-26. Decision table "Eligibility"

AUTHOR. Any comments?

READER. Both these decision tables are simple, but they use "Risk Category" that we've already defined in our library. The goal "Eligibility" also depends on the subgoal "Affordability", for which we have two decision modes in the library. As we deal with pre-bureau processing, I believe we should use the decision model "Affordability" defined by the file "Decisions/Affordability/DecisionModelPreBureau.xls".

AUTHOR. You are making all the good points. Please note that our decision model "Affordability" already includes the decision model "Risk Category" – see Fig. 6-20. It means the Environment table for the decision model "Bureau Strategy" inside the file "DecisionModel.xls" will look as follows:

Environment	
include	Rules.xls
	../Affordability/DecisionModelPreBureau.xls

Fig. 6-27. The Environment table Bureau Strategy

What else do you need to do to finalize the decision model "Bureau Strategy"?

READER. First of all, we need to add missing 3 decision variables "Eligibility", "Bureau Call Type", and "Bureau Strategy" to our common glossary. They all belong to the business concept

"Application". We also need to adjust the settings in the file "Decisions/BureauStrategy/build.bat" as in Fig. 6-28.

```
set GOAL="Bureau Strategy"
set INPUT_FILE_NAME=repository/Decisions/BureauStrategy/DecisionModel.xls
set OUTPUT_FILE_NAME=repository/Decisions/BureauStrategy/Goals.xls
```

Fig. 6-28. File "build.bat" for Bureau Strategy

AUTHOR. Double-Click on this file will generate "Goals.xls" in the same folder "BureauStrategy". Let's look at this automatically generated execution path:

Decision DecisionBureauStrategy
ActionExecute
Decision Tables
ApplicationRiskScore
PreBureauRiskCategory
PMT
RequiredMonthlyInstallment
DisposableIncome
CreditContingencyFactor
Affordability
Eligibility
BureauCallType
BureauStrategy

Fig. 6-29. Automatically generated execution path for Bureau Strategy

READER. Yes! It actually shows the execution sequence of all subgoals starting with "ApplicationRiskScore" and ending up with "BureauStrategy". How OpenRules could figure this out?

AUTHOR. OpenRules implements a special algorithm that goes through all decision tables, recursively identifies all goals and variables which they depend on, and then resolves all dependencies to come up with an execution path similar to the one in Fig. 6-29.

READER. It's really cool that OpenRules automatically resolves all dependencies between goals and subgoals.

AUTHOR. So, after all, it was relatively easy to build the decision model "Bureau Strategy" using our library of already defined decision models. Now we can similarly assemble the decision model for the goal "Routing".

Assembling Decision Model "Routing"

Here are the routing rules extracted from the DMN specification:

If	If	If	If	Then
DecisionTable Routing				
Affordability	Bankrupt	Risk Category	Credit Score	Routing
FALSE				DECLINE
TRUE	TRUE			DECLINE
TRUE		DECLINE		DECLINE
TRUE	FALSE	HIGH		REFER
TRUE			<580	REFER
TRUE			>=580	ACCEPT

Fig. 6-30. Decision table "Routing"

This table uses the same decision variables "Risk Category" and "Affordability" but for post-bureau processing. It means our Environment table in the file "DecisionModel.xls" should look as below:

Environment	
include	Rules.xls
	../Affordability/DecisionModelPostBureau.xls

Fig. 6-31. The Environment table for Routing

I will add the variables "Credit Score" and "Routing" to the business concept "Application" and the variable "Bankrupt" to the business concept "BureauData" inside our common glossary. And here is the corresponding file "build.bat":

```
set GOAL="Routing"
set INPUT_FILE_NAME=repository/Decisions/Routing/DecisionModel.xls
set OUTPUT_FILE_NAME=repository/Decisions/Routing/Goals.xls
```

Fig. 6-32. File "build.bat" for Routing

AUTHOR. If you build and run both decision models "Bureau Strategy" and "Routing" using the downloadable OpenRules project "LoanOrigination", you will see that both models produce the expected results. So, we quite easily assembled these decision models taking advantage of the already defined library of smaller decision models for the loan origination domain.

Decision Model Assembly Steps

READER. I like when you say "assembled" – it feels that we are at the Decision Modeling Factory.

AUTHOR. Wow, what a nice term! If you don't mind, I will use it in my blog. Here are the "**assembly steps**":

1. Implement business logic using decision tables in the file "Rules.xls"
2. Create the Environment table in the file "DecisionModel.xls" that may refer to the already implemented decision models
3. Add new decision variables to the common Glossary
4. Adjust "build.bat" to automatically generate an execution path in the file "Goals.xls"
5. Create and run test cases for the decision model.

Assembling Decision Model "Loan Origination Result"

AUTHOR. At the end of today's session, I want us to build a top-level decision model that produces the ultimate "Loan Origination Result". It will also give us an opportunity to learn one more decision model integration method.

According to the initial business process in Fig. 6-1 there could be 3 possible loan origination results: ACCEPT, DECLINE, and REFER. It's only natural to present business logic presented in Fig. 6-1 as a decision table:

DecisionTable LoanOriginationResult				
Condition		Condition		Action
Bureau Strategy		Routing		Loan Origination Result
Is	DECLINE			DECLINE
Is One Of		Is	DECLINE	DECLINE
Is One Of	BUREAU,THROUGH	Is	REFER	REFER
Is One Of		Is	ACCEPT	ACCEPT

Fig. 6-33. Determining Loan Origination Result

As usual, I put this decision table in the file "Rules.xls" in the folder "repository/Decisions/LoanOriginationResult". What else should we do to assemble this decision model?

READER. We should add "Loan Origination Result" to the business concept "Application".

AUTHOR. OK. The finalized glossary is presented in Fig. 6-34. What else?

READER. As we see in Fig. 6-33, the decision goal "Loan Origination Result" depends on already defined goals "Bureau Strategy" and "Routing". We probably should modify the file "DecisionModel.xls" for this model by updating its Environment table as we did previously.

Dialog-Session 6

Variable	Business Concept	Attribute
Age		age
Marital Status		maritalStatus
Employment Status		employmentStatus
Monthly Income	Applicant	monthlyIncome
Monthly Repayments		monthlyRepayments
Monthly Expenses		monthlyExpenses
Existing Customer		existingCustomer
Application Risk Score		applicationRiskScore
Risk Category		riskCategory
PMT		pmt
Required Monthly Installment		requiredMonthlyInstallment
Disposable Income		disposableIncome
Credit Contingency Factor		creditContingencyFactor
Affordability	Application	affordability
Eligibility		eligibility
Bureau Call Type		bureauCallType
Bureau Strategy		bureauStrategy
Routing		routing
Loan Origination Result		routing
Product Type		productType
Amount		amount
Rate	RequestedProduct	rate
Term		term
Bureau Name		bureauName
Bankrupt	BureauData	bankrupt
Credit Score		creditScore

Fig. 6-34. Finalized Common Glossary

AUTHOR. So, you'll need to include references to both files:

- ../BureauStrategy/DecisionModel.xls
- ../Routing/DecisionModel.xls.

READER. Yes, because our model will use both decision model "Bureau Strategy" and "Routing".

AUTHOR. However, they both use the decision variable "Risk Strategy" and OpenRules would not know which one to use and it will produce the proper errors when you try to build the model.

READER. I am afraid you are right. So, what can we do to still reuse already created decision models?

Decision Model Assembly Techniques: "Include" vs "Import"

AUTHOR. Don't worry. OpenRules provides another integration method to be used when decision variables with the same names are used by different subgoals of one main goal. It's called "**Decision Model Import**". Instead of "including" decision models in the same Environment table, we may "import" them using a special table of the type "DecisionImport". For example, in our case we may add the following table to the file "LoanOriginationResult/DecisionModel.xls":

DecisionImport decisionImports	
Imported Decision File	Decision Name
file:repository/Decisions/BureauStrategy/Goals.xls	DecisionBureauStrategy
file:repository/Decisions/Routing/Goals.xls	DecisionRouting

Fig. 6-35. Importing Decision Models

In this case, OpenRules will handle each of our 3 decision models "Loan Origination Result", "Bureau Strategy" and "Routing" as separate decision services. Internally, it will create a separate instance of OpenRules Engine for each imported decision model but it's not important for you. What is important that such importing of decision models prevents possible name clashes even when they use decision variables with the same names.

READER. OK, I am glad that we still can reuse our already created decision models. And how the Environment table for "Loan Origination Result" will look like now?

AUTHOR. Here it is:

Environment	
include	Rules.xls
	../Glossary/Glossary.xls

Fig. 6-36. The Environment table for Loan Origination Result

READER. I see we still need to refer to Glossary but not to any imported decision models. That's good.

AUTHOR. You only need to adjust the file "build.bat" using GOAL="Loan Origination Result". When you double-click on "build.bat" it will generate "Goals.xls" with the following execution path:

Decision DecisionLoanOriginationResult
ActionExecute
Decision Tables
DecisionBureauStrategy
DecisionRouting
LoanOriginationResult

Fig. 6-37. The generated execution path for Loan Origination Result

Please note that this path does not expand the execution paths for the imported models "BureauStrategy" and "Routing". Fig. 6-38 shows you an example of the execution results. As you can see, Risk Category was calculated as HIGH for pre-bureau processing, and as LOW for post-bureau processing. Some calculations were done twice but the total execution time is just 188 milliseconds.

```
RUN TEST: Test 3
Execute DecisionBureauStrategy
Execute ApplicationRiskScore
  Conclusion: Application Risk Score = 0
  Conclusion: Application Risk Score += 35
  Conclusion: Application Risk Score += 80
  Conclusion: Application Risk Score += 98
Execute PreBureauRiskCategory
  Assign: Risk Category = HIGH
Execute PMT
  Assign: PMT = 4083.066538617192
Execute RequiredMonthlyInstallment
  Assign: Required Monthly Installment = 4108.066538617191
Execute DisposableIncome
  Assign: Disposable Income = 3900.0
Execute CreditContingencyFactor
  Assign: Credit Contingency Factor = 0.6
Execute Affordability
  Assign: Affordability = false
Execute Eligibility
  Assign: Eligibility = INELIGIBLE
Execute BureauCallType
  Assign: Bureau Call Type = FULL
Execute BureauStrategy
  Assign: Bureau Strategy = DECLINE
Execute DecisionRouting
Execute PMT
  Assign: PMT = 4083.066538617192
Execute RequiredMonthlyInstallment
  Assign: Required Monthly Installment = 4108.066538617191
Execute DisposableIncome
  Assign: Disposable Income = 3900.0
Execute ApplicationRiskScore
  Conclusion: Application Risk Score = 0
  Conclusion: Application Risk Score += 35
  Conclusion: Application Risk Score += 80
  Conclusion: Application Risk Score += 98
Execute PostBureauRiskCategory
  Assign: Risk Category = LOW
Execute CreditContingencyFactor
  Assign: Credit Contingency Factor = 0.8
Execute Affordability
  Assign: Affordability = false
Execute Routing
  Assign: Routing = DECLINE
Execute LoanOriginationResult
  Assign: Loan Origination Result = DECLINE
Validating results for the test <Test 3>
Test 3 was successful
Executed test Test 3 in 188 ms
```

Fig. 6-38. The Execution Results for Loan Origination Result

READER. Yes, now I see all executed goals and subgoals with the intermediate results.

AUTHOR. The explanation of all actually executed rules can be found in this HTML-report.

Knowledge Repository Organization

And finally, I want you to look at our knowledge repository:

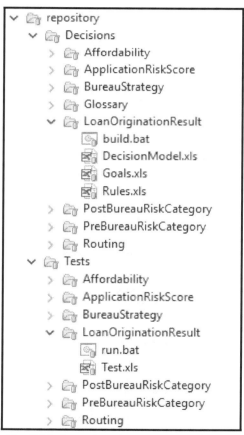

Fig. 6-39. Repository's Decisions and Tests

All decision models are in the folder "**repository**" with two main sub-folders "**Decisions**" and "**Tests**" expanded as below:

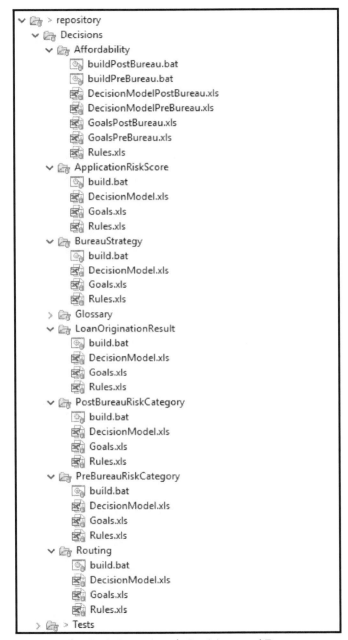

Fig. 6-40. Repository's Decisions and Tests

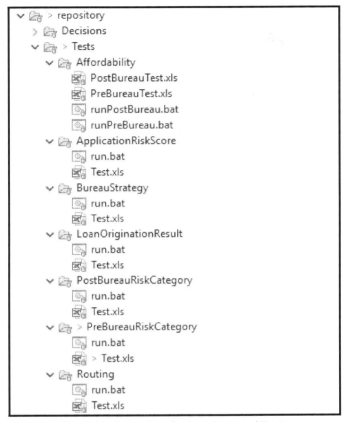

Fig. 6-41. Repository's Decisions and Tests

All decision models have a similar organization: DecisionModel.xls, Rules.xls, Goals.xls, and build.bat. All files such as "Goals.xls" were generated automatically. Of course, larger decision models can contain more xls-files which should be referenced from the Environment table of their files "DecisionModel.xls". All test cases are in sub-folders of the folder "**Tests**" under the same names as the corresponding decision models. In the real-world decision management systems, it is extremely important to maintain both: decision models and their tests! Such a parallel organization of the knowledge repository provides a good example of how to do it.

READER. I believe it was also critically important to create and maintain a common business glossary in the file "repository/Decisions/Glossary/Glossary.xls".

AUTHOR. Yes, we started with a small Glossary that kept growing as we added more decision models. This glossary serves as a spine that keeps all surrounding decision models together.

READER. Thank you. As always, it was a very productive session. Now I am eager to start building my own decision models.

Summing Up

It's time for us to sum up. We applied the goal-oriented approach to decision modeling. Today we demonstrated this approach using relatively complex decision problems from one business domain. We created a library of smaller decision models and used them to assemble new decision models. All decision models have been tested independently. We've learned two integration methods ("include" and "import") that allowed us to incorporate low-level decision models into top-level decision models. And like for all our previous sessions, everything was done in Excel using OpenRules as an integrated decision modeling and execution tool.

I hope now you are ready to start building business decision models for your company, which will be highly efficient, self-explanatory, and ready for future changes and enhancements. If you have any problems, you always may contact support@openrules.com to get immediate and constructive advice. Good luck and Happy Decision Modeling!

References

1. Standard "Decision Model and Notation (DMN)", Object Management Group

2. Catalog of DMN Supporting Tools http://openjvm.jvmhost.net/DMNtools/

3. OpenRules, Open Source Business Rules and Decision Management System, http://openrules.com

4. DMN in Action with OpenRules by Jacob Feldman, 2017

5. DMN Cookbook by Bruce Silver and Edson Tirelli, 2018

6. Real-World Decision Modeling with DMN by James Taylor and Jan Purchase, 2016

7. DMN Method and Style: The Practitioner's Guide to Decision Modeling with Business Rules by Bruce Silver, 2016

8. Knowledge Automation: How to Implement Decision Management in Business Processes by Alan N. Fish, 2012

9. The Decision Model by Barbara von Halle, Larry Goldberg, 2010

10. The History of Modeling Decisions using Tables by Jan Vanthienen, 2012

11. Decision Management Community, http://DMCommunity.org

12. Business Rules Community, http://BRCommunity.com

Made in the USA
Coppell, TX
03 August 2022

80868901R00097